OPTIONS TRADING FOR BEGINNERS:

THE MARKET GUIDE ON HOW TO START INVESTING FOR A LIVING WITH TECHNICAL ANALYSIS USING DAY & SWING TECHNIQUES. MAKE MONEY AND GAIN FINANCIAL FREEDOM (STOCK, PSYCHOLOGY)

The content contained within this book may not be reproduced, duplicated or transmitted without direct written permission from the author or the publisher.

Under no circumstances will any blame or legal responsibility be held against the publisher, or author, for any damages, reparation, or monetary loss due to the information contained within this book. Either directly or indirectly.

Legal Notice:

This book is copyright protected. This book is only for personal use. You cannot amend, distribute, sell, use, quote or paraphrase any part, or the content within this book, without the consent of the author or publisher.

Disclaimer Notice:

Please note the information contained within this document is for educational and entertainment purposes only. All effort has been executed to present accurate, up to date, and reliable, complete information. No warranties of any kind are declared or implied. Readers acknowledge that the author is not engaging in the rendering of legal, financial, medical or professional advice. The content within this book has been derived from various sources. Please consult a licensed professional before attempting any techniques outlined in this book.

By reading this document, the reader agrees that under no circumstances is the author responsible for any losses, direct or indirect, which are incurred as a result of the use of the information contained within this document, including, but not limited to, — errors, omissions, or inaccuracies.

Table of Contents

Introduction

People trade options to profit off price moves on the stock market. That is, traders use the method of buying low and selling high to make profits from trades.

You can buy options that expire at various dates in the future. Most of the action is centered on options that expire within a week to a month, but some options expire several weeks, months, and even years into the future. As we'll see, the expiration date for the option is something you'll need to pay close attention to.

But for small investors, one of the best things about options is the high return on investment or ROI!

So options trading is more accessible that day or swing trading stocks because of the low capital amounts required to get started, and you'll earn a much higher ROI!

Being successful in trading requires hard work and a lot of studying, and this concept applies not only to option trading but to all financial actions of this kind. Be mindful about time scales in options trading, and remember that in the first few days or a few weeks you won't see any dramatic shifts in the value of your options. The reason for this is the fact that the trading profit actually comes from the loss of other traders. The way of getting profit is the same whether you trade derivatives, shares or options. The amount of money that goes around is smaller when you reduce the commissions that dealers and brokers take. These amounts of money are one of the reasons why many traders lose during the trade. You should educate yourself to avoid the fate of most of these brokers. Learn how to trade more smartly, as it will help you thrive or, at worst, to survive in the trading market. Consider these next pages simply as a start of your options trading journey in which you will be able to recognize and define the basic terms and strategies for your future career. It should give you the grounding that you need and motivate you to search forward and educate yourself further.

Well, I hope you are as excited about trading options as I am. Let's go ahead and get started!

Chapter 1 What Are Stock Options?

What Are Stock Options

We need to get an understanding of the meaning of stock options. We first have to know the meaning of the two words independently.

Stock refers to:

☐ The total money a company has from selling shares to individuals.

☐ A portion of the ownership of the company that can be sold to members of the public

Option (finance) refers to:

☐ A contract that provides the buyer with the right, though not any obligation, of selling or buying an asset for a given agreed strike price at a specified date based on the type of option

Now that we know the meaning of both stocks and options, we can easily define stock options. We can define the term in the following ways:

Stock options provide an investor with the right to sell or buy a stock at a set price and date.

The stock option can also refer to an advantage in the form of an opportunity provided by a company to any employee to buy shares in a company at an agreed-upon fixed price or a discount.

Stock options have been a topic of interest in recent years. We are having more and more people engaging in options trading. The profitability of stock options has resulted in a lot of debates. Some say it's a scam; others claim that it is not a worthy investment while others say that they are minting millions from it. All these speculations draw us to one direction, which is; understanding what stock options are. To accurately answer this question, we will have to go through stock options keenly. We will be required to know all about it and what it entails. This information makes it easy to make judgments with actual facts as opposed to using assumptions. You will get to say something that you can actually back up. Having knowledge gives you an added advantage and places you in a powerful position.

As a novice trader, acquiring information will transform your trading abilities. Having the necessary skills and knowledge will make you an expert in trading within a matter of time. This book will provide you with the knowledge you need before engaging in a stock option. It is a good thing that you have taken the first step in getting this book. It indicates that you are ready and will to learn, and that is a major move. Asides from acquiring knowledge, it is crucial that you learn to implement it. This will mean practically doing that which you have learnt. Some people acquire knowledge, but they are unable to utilize it for their own benefit effectively. I hope that after you go through the book, you will have the courage to trade a stock option. This book mainly addresses the beginners, and it is written to make a difference in their life. I will proceed to take you through stock options and make you aware of what it entails.

Understanding Stock Options

For us to understand stock options, we consider the following:

Strike Price

For one to know if a stock can be exercised, they will need to consider the strike price. By the time an option gets to the expiration date, there is a price that it is expected to have. This price should be lower or higher than the stock price, and it is what we refer to as the strike price of an underlying asset. If as an investor, you predict that the stock's value will increase, you can purchase a call option at the set strike price. When it comes to putting options, the strike price will be the price at which an asset is traded by the option buyer by the time the contract expires. The strike price can also be referred to as the exercise price. It is a major factor to consider while establishing the option value. Depending on when the options are carried out, the strike price will differ. As an investor, it is good to keep track of the strike price since it helps in identifying the quality of an investment.

Styles

There are two main option styles. These are European and American options styles. If you intend to engage in options trading, it is advisable to equip yourself with knowledge of the various styles. As you analyze the styles, you will identify those that work for you and those that do not. You will also find that some styles are easier to learn and handle as opposed to others. You can decide to engage in the one that is convenient for you and avoid engaging in the style that you have difficulties understanding.

The American style option allows one to exercise a trade any period between the time of purchase and the time a contract expires. Most traders engage in this style due to its convenience. It allows one to carry out a trade any period within which a contract is considered to be valid. The European style option is not commonly used as compared to the American style. In the European option style, a trader can only exercise their options during the expiration date. If you are not an expert in options trading, I would advise you to avoid using the European style.

Expiration date

An expiration date refers to the period in which a contract is regarded as worthless. Stocks have expiration dates. The period between when they were purchased and the expiry date, indicate the validity of an option. As a trader, you are expected to utilize the contracts to your advantage, within this time frame. You can trade as much as you can and get high returns within the period of buying and the period of expiry. Learn to utilize the time provided adequately. If you are not careful, the option may expire before you get a chance to exercise it.

We have may beginners who assume this factor and end up making heavy losses. You will be required to be keen while engaging in the stock market. Forgetting to look into the expiry date may result in your stocks being regarded as worthless without getting a chance of investing in them. In some rare cases, the stocks are exercised during the expiry date. This is common in the European option. I would not encourage a beginner to engage in this type of option. It is tricky and could lead to a loss if you are not careful while carrying out the trade.

Contacts

Contracts refer to the amount of shares an investor is intending to purchase. One hundred shares of an underlying asset are equal to one contract. Contracts aid in establishing the stock's value. Contracts tend to be valuable before the expiry date. After the expiry date, a contract can be regarded as worthless. Knowing this will help you discover the best time to exercise a contract. In a case where a trader purchases ten contracts, he or she gets to 10 $ 350 calls. When the stock prices go above $ 350, at the expiry trade, the trader gets the chance to buy or sell 1000 shares of their stock at $350. This happens regardless of the stock price at that particular time. In an event whereby the stock is lower than $350, the option will expire worthlessly. This will result in making a complete loss as an investor. You will lose the whole amount you used to purchase options, and there is no way of getting it back. If you intend to invest in options trading, it is good to become aware of the contracts and how you can exercise them for a profitable options trading outcome.

Premium

The premium refers to the money used to purchase options. You can obtain the premium by multiplying the call price and the number of contracts by 100. The '100' is the number of shares per contract. This is more like the investment made by the trader expecting great returns. While investing, you will expect that the investment you chose to engage in will result in a profitable outcome. No one gets in business anticipating a loss. You find that one is always hopeful that the investment they have chosen to engage in will be beneficial. You will constantly look forward to getting the best out of a trade.

The above factors tell us more about stocks. In case you were stuck and didn't fully understand what stocks entail, now you have a better understanding. You will come across numerous terms when you decide to engage in stocks. Do not let the terms scare you; they are mostly things you knew, but just didn't know that they go by those terms. We have many people who are quite investing in stocks, just because they could not understand the various terms being used. This should not be the case. You can take some time to go through the terms and understand what they entail carefully.

Options in Stock Market

Stock options are not as hard as people make them appear. At times people try to make them seem difficult, yet it is an easy thing that can be grasped by almost everyone. As a beginner, do not be discouraged into thinking that options trading is a difficult investment. You will be surprised how easy it is, and you will wonder why you never invested in it sooner. When engaging in stock options, there are four factors the investors will have to consider. Putting these factors into consideration will have a positive impact on their trade.

The Right, But Not the Obligation

What comes in your mind when you read this statement? Well, when we talk or rights, we mean that you have the freedom to purchase a certain type of option. When we talk of obligation, we are referring to the fact that one does not have a legal authority to exercise a duty. Options do not give traders a legal authority to carry out a duty. This means that there is freedom to trade, but it is not legally mandated.

Buying or Selling

As a trader, you are given the right to purchase or trade an option. There are two types of stock that one can choose from. We have the put option and the call option. Both differ and have their individual pros and cons. If you intend trading in options, it is important that you equip yourself with adequate knowledge before trading or purchasing stocks. This information will have an impact on your expected income. The stocks you choose to buy or sell will dictate if you will earn high returns or if you will end up making a loss.

Set Price

There is a certain price that has been set to exercise the option. The price will vary depending on the option type. Some stock options tend to be valued more than other options. There are a number of factors that will influence the price of options. As you continue reading this book, you will come across those factors. Knowing them will help you know when to carry out a trade, and when not to carry out a trade, depending on the influence of the factors; a trade may generate a high income or end up resulting in a loss.

Expiry Date

The expiry date is when a contract will be considered useless. Stock options have an expiry date. The date is set to determine the option's value. Any period before the expiration date, a contact is regarded as being valid. This means that it can be utilized to generate income at any point before the expiry date. When it gets to the expiry date, a trader has no power to exercise the option. This is as a result of the contract being regarded as worthless. As an investor, it is good to constantly ensure that your investment is within the duration of its validity.

Top Reasons to Trade Options

We've seen that trading options are an activity that has its upsides and its downsides. In this chapter, we are going to look at the top reasons that you want to trade options. Keep in mind that you can personalize your portfolio and investment strategy, so it's not necessary to go "all in" when it comes to trading options. You can have options trading as one part of a diverse investment strategy. In fact, many people use options to cover risks in other parts of their overall portfolio.

Trading Options provides an investment opportunity with limited capital

Take a situation where we began with an example showing that for $250, you could control 100 shares of stock that would cost someone $3,900 to buy outright. We then expanded on that and saw what kind of possibilities existed when investing larger amounts. However, if you are just starting out with investing, it's not necessary to buy more than one options contract at a time. You can invest for a relatively small amount of money depending on the stock. Trading doesn't have to be approached with an all or nothing mentality. You can start with small investments and work your way up by reinvesting your profits.

You can hedge your risks with index funds

Most people who invest in stocks will be investing in index funds in order to have a diversified portfolio. By utilizing options, you can hedge your risks with index funds. Index puts can help you mitigate losses if the market experiences a major downturn. Smart investors will utilize index puts so that the next recession doesn't leave them with huge losses.

Profit off of other losses

OK, it sounds bad when phrased that way. You can use puts to profit from downturns in stock prices. This is an opportunity that simply isn't available when doing regular stock trading.

Collect Premiums

As we'll see, there are ways to profit from doing so, but no matter what, you can pocket the premiums. This is another way to earn money in an overall investment portfolio that uses diverse strategies as well as diverse investments.

Capitalize on outsized gains

One of the biggest benefits that come with trading options is being able to control large amounts of stock that could have a huge upside if there is a major increase in stock price by purchasing a large number of call options. Of course, being a fortune teller isn't generally a lucrative income, but you can increase your chances of success by carefully studying the markets and the companies behind the individual stocks. Look for dynamic areas where new companies could see a huge gain in the stock price over a short period. The risk is that you'll lose your premium if the strike price isn't surpassed, but if it is then you'll have a chance to score big. We already showed a simple example with a return on investment of 140%, but it's even possible to get an ROI of 500% or even more.

Options are flexible

When you are working with options, you will find that you get a ton of flexibility. You can choose to buy or sell, you can go with different expiration dates, you can pick from a variety of strategies and assets, and you can even have control over your strike price. There are even ways that you will be able to profit if the market goes down. Sometimes all this flexibility is going to make working in options more complicated, but if you know what you are doing, this type of flexibility will help you to profit, regardless of how the market is doing.

Gain leverage

Another benefit you will be able to get when you decide to work with the options market is the idea of leverage. To keep things simple, leverage is a big advantage to the trader. When you gain leverage, you are giving yourself more options because you are able to put more money into the market without needing to have more startup capital to help you out. This can be dangerous because it causes you to lose more money than you have in the beginning, but if you are careful and read the market right, it will make you earn a ton more money even with lower startup costs.

Chapter 2 How option trading works

There are several parties involved in a trade. It isn't possible to trade directly with everyone, and it isn't even practical. This is why, for the sake of convenience, stock exchanges were formed. This is a channel where all the stocks are being traded.

You cannot work directly with the stock exchange as this would create great confusion. It would mean too many people making deals at the same time. This is where brokers come into play.

Brokers work as the mediators, as the channel of communication between you and the exchange. They charge a commission for their service. In the stock exchange industry's early stages, most of the transactions were carried out by the brokers on behalf of their clients. Brokers nowadays still carry out transactions on behalf of their clients, but the clients now have the option to manage their accounts easily. You will have to open a trading account with a broker, and the broker will give you access to that trading account.

Currently, a number of software programs have been successfully developed where you can directly trade on stock exchanges. The program recommendation, as well as the access credentials, will be provided by the brokerage firm you'll choose.

Like a bond or stock, an option is a tradable security. You can purchase or sell options to a foreign broker or trade them on an exchange within the United States. An option may give you the opportunity to leverage your cash, though it may be high risk because it eventually expires *(expiration date).* For stock options, each option contract represents 100 shares.

An instance of an option is if you want to buy a car/house, but for whatever reason, do not have immediate cash for it but will get the cash next month. You can now buy the asset at the agreed price and sell it for a profit. The value of the asset may also depreciate perhaps when the house develops plumbing problems or other problems or in the case of a vehicle, gets into an accident. If you decide not to buy the asset and let your purchase option expire, you lose your initial investment, the $2,500 you placed for the option.

This is the general concept of how option trading happens; however, in reality, option trading is a lot more complex and involves more risks.

What kind of investor are you?

Trading has its strategies, its techniques and its secrets. Different things apply to different people. What works for someone else may not work for you. Why? Because you are two different kinds of investors. Aggressive personalities invest in a completely different manner than conservative personalities. People who are not afraid to take risks are completely different investors than those who are methodical and play it safe. There is no better or worse here. It is just the style of doing business.

There are two major categories of investors:

The active investor Those are also called traders. They do not hold on to options for a long time and their interest lies in making profit from the volatility of the prices. The trade a lot and as often as possible.

The passive investor These are also called the buy-and-hold investors. They are the exact opposites. They are interested in making the maximum gain from each option and they do not trade often. And when they do they will trade once or twice.

Most people could find themselves at any point between those two categories. Some tend to be more aggressive, others tend to be slightly more conservative. One would think that being in the middle would offer you the best of both. But this is not always the case.

Aggressive personalities are actually impatient personalities. For them patience is not a virtue. So if you force them to trade conservatively in most cases they do not even know how. And they do not care to learn. The same holds true for the conservative people. Forcing them to trade more options than one or two, creates a chaos in their mindset.

Each one balances to whichever side they feel more comfortable. The side that will allow him or her to think straight and make the proper decisions. That would be the perfect world, but unfortunately there are always strings attached.

Even the most conservative investor may have to act fast and trade all his options should an emergency arise. An aggressive person should learn that there are cases where trading may be forbidden, or banned, or halted for some reason and they will have to hold on to their options.

The deeper you get into options trading the wiser you become. No matter what kind of investor you may be, the market itself will teach you, sometimes the hard way (i.e. it will cost you a lot of money) when it is time to hold on to an option and when it is time to trade it.

Chapter 3 Types of Options

There are several types of options that are commonly traded. These options can be categorized into various forms with respect to the features they possess. The brad sense of options has two major types of options. The two options are known as puts and call options. A call option has the ability to give a buyer the right to purchase a financial instrument. On the other hand, options hand an individual the right to sell the asset. There is a clear distinction that is used to classify the option, which is it's either they are European style or American style. The notion you can end up having is that the classification is done on the basis of geographical location, which is not the case. The factual truth is that the classification is done because of where the contract has the potential of being exercised.

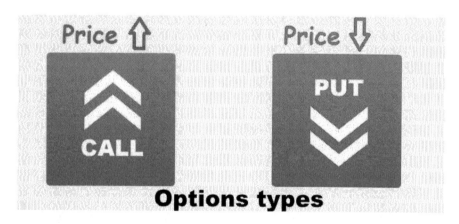

Options types

The process of classification of the option goes a notch further to using the method used in trading to classify them. Other methods used to distinguish the existing types of options include the underlying security they relate to and the expiration cycle that they contain. This broadens individual findings to several types of options that exist across the globe. These types of options can be well expounded for an individual to understand the concept of trade options. They include;

Calls Options

These types of options are characterized by giving an individual the right to purchase the agreed asset on a future date. The assets being purchased tend to have an already agreed-upon price. There are certain situations that can make an individual make a call on an asset. The most common situation is when one speculates that the asset will improve in its worth over a certain period of time. A characteristic of calls is that they have an expiry date, which is dependent on the contract a person has entered in to. The asset being targeted can be bought before the expiration date.

Puts Options

Puts are always the exact opposite of calls kind of options. An individual who owns the put option has the right bestowed to him of selling the underlying assets. The process of selling tends to have an agreed price that has been determined for the future act. This scenario happens during intriguing phases in the financial markets. An individual is likely to fall under put action when he or she has speculated the value of the assets to fall. Despite being the opposite of the call, there are similarities between calls and puts. A similar major occurrence is that they are both limited to the time set. Therefore, puts have an expiration date on the contract one has entered.

American Style Options

The American style has nothing related to buying and selling of contracts when it narrows down to options. It focuses its lenses on the terms that are stated in the contractual terms in an agreement. Basic knowledge at this point is that options come with an expiration date in their contracts, which gives a trader in the financial markets the right of either buying or selling an underlying asset. In the American style option, an individual has the right to exercise his or her contract prior to the expiration date in the contract. The stated flexibility tends to advantage to a trader using American style options.

European Style Options

Individuals who are afforded this type of options are not given the same flexibility that is experienced by people who are using American style contracts. The timeline in this type of option is very strict. An individual using European style contracts is supposed to only trade his or her underlying assets on the date of expiration and not before or after.

Exchange-Traded Options

It is also commonly known as listed options across the globe to several financial market participants. It can be termed as one of the most common types of options known to people. There are several option contracts that are listed in the on public trading exchanges. These are the kinds of options that are referred to as exchange trade options. They can be able to be bought or sold by anyone with the aid of subtle brokers.

Over the Counter Options

This kind of trade options is only traded in the over the counter markets. These common characteristics that compound over the counter trade options make them not easily accessible to the entirety of the public. The terms of contracts in these forms of trade options tend to be complicated compared to other forms of trade options.

Employee Stock Option

This form of stock options is known to be presented to employees. An employee of a certain company offering option can be granted this contract by the company he or she is working for. Their general use is to facilitate remuneration to employees. It goes ahead to act as bonuses or incentives employees of a specific company are given. It has several advantages since it attracts people to work for organizations that offer such.

Cash Settled Options

These kinds of contracts do not characterize themselves with the physical transfer of the traded assets. What is takes place in a cash-settled option can be related to the name it possesses. Profits that are made in this kind of option are settled in cash forms to the winning party. There are certain reasons that befall this type of option trading. It comes to the occurrence when the asset being transferred is expensive or complicated to be transferred to the other party.

Types of Options Based on Expiration

Contracts have the possibility of being classified according to their expiration dates. This relates to certain phenomena that a trader is supposed to be able to sell with respect to the set date in a contract. The contacts agreed that options trading tends to differ with the cycles they possess. They include;

• Regular Options; they are based on the cycles the trade is agreed upon and listed in the contracts. One is likely to have four expiration months to choose in a financial year.

• Weekly Options; they were introduced in the year 2005 and are also known as weeklies. They have the same principles as regular options thought they had reduced timings in them. Weeklies tend to be used in limited financial instruments.

- Quarterly Options; they listed in the exchange markets with their expiration dates being similar or near to financial quarters. Some people term them as weeklies, and they expire on the last day of expiration.

Types of Options by the Underlying Security

A stock option is a general that has been the focus when people tend to talk about trade options. This is where the underlying assets of accompanying are publicly listed can be used as a financial instrument. It is common knowledge of people who have invested in this form of trade. There are several kinds of options that are involved in this case, and they include;

- **Stock Options;** A company that is publicly listed has its shares is, they form underlying assets that are being traded in this contract.

- **Index Options;** They tend to have a close similarity to the stock options. However, there is a difference that depicts the blurred line. The split comes when the underlying form of security being traded is not stocks; rather. They are a company's indexes.

- **Currency Options;** This contract has a clear difference from other forms of option. It is because it gives a trader the right to either sell or buy currency. The trade is made at agreed terms of the contract.

- **Future Options;** The future contract is the underlying asset used in this form of options trading. A future Options has the potential of giving a trader a right to participate in a future contract.

- **Commodity Option;** The asset which is underlined in this kind of option trading tends to be a physical commodity.

- **Basket Option;** It is a kind of option trading that has several financial instruments as the underlying assets.

Exotic Options

It is a term that is used to characterize those options contracts that have been customized by options traders. The resulting effect of this customization makes the contracts to be more complex. They are termed as Non-Standardized options in some cases. They are additional exotic contracts that are only found in the OTC markets. However, there are some of these options contracts that have started being famous in the current financial markets. These options include:

• Barrier Options; a pay-out is always given to a holder of this form of contract until the moments the price stated in this contract reaches.

• Binary Options; the owner of the underlying financial assets is given a fixed amount of money in the event the contract expires.

• Chooser Options; these form of trade options allows a financial trader to choose whether to call or put at any time.

• Compound Options; a form of trading option in which the underlying financial asset is another option.

Chapter 4 The Basics of Options Contracts

In this chapter, we will introduce the concept of options contracts and how they are used in the stock market. In our introductory discussion, we will be focusing on the most basic way to get involved in options, which involves buying options contracts based on bets you make on whether future stock prices will rise or fall. Later we will see that you can also write or sell options contracts and that the contracts themselves are traded on the markets.

What is an Options Contract?

An options contract sounds fancy but it's a pretty simple concept.

- It's a contract. That means it's a legal agreement between a buyer and a seller.

- It gives the purchaser of the contract the opportunity to purchase or dispose of an asset with a fixed amount.

- The purchase is optional – so the buyer of the contract does not have to buy or sell the asset.

- The contract has an expiration date, so the purchaser – if they choose to exercise their right – must make the trade on or before the expiration date.

- The purchaser of the contract pays a non-refundable fee for the contract.

While the focus of this book is on options contracts related to the stock market, there are options contracts that take place in all aspects of daily life including real estate and speculation. A simple example illustrates the concept of an options contract.

Suppose you are itching to buy a BMW and you've decided the model you want must be silver. You drop by a local dealer and it turns out they don't have a silver model in stock. The dealer claims he can get you one by the end of the month. You say you'll take the car if the dealer can get it by the last day of the month and he'll sell it to you for $67,500. He agrees and requires you to put a $3,000 deposit on the car.

If the last day of the month arrives and the dealer hasn't produced the car, then you're freed from the contract and get your money back. In the event he does produce the car at any date before the end of the month, you have the option to buy it or not. If you really wanted the car you can buy it, but of course, you can't be forced to buy the car, and maybe you've changed your mind in the interim.

The right is there but not the obligation to purchase, in short, no pressure if you decided not to push through with the purchase of the car. If you decide to let the opportunity pass, however, since the dealer met his end of the bargain and produced the car, you lose the $3,000 deposit.

In this case, the dealer, who plays the role of the writer of the contract, *has the obligation to follow through with the sale* based upon the agreed upon price.

Suppose that when the car arrives at the dealership, BMW announces it will no longer make silver cars. As a result, prices of new silver BMWs that were the last ones to roll off the assembly line, skyrocket. Other dealers are selling their silver BMWs for $100,000. However, since this dealer entered into an options contract with you, he must sell the car to you for the pre-agreed price of $67,500. You decide to get the car and drive away smiling, knowing that you saved $32,500 and that you could sell it at a profit if you wanted to.

The situation here is capturing the essence of options contracts, even if you've never thought of haggling with a car dealer in those terms.

An option is in a sense a kind of bet. In the example of the car, the bet is that the dealer can produce the exact car you want within the specified time period and at the agreed upon price. The dealer is betting too. His bet is that the pre-agreed to price is a good one for him. Of course, if BMW stops making silver cars, then he's made the wrong bet.

It can work the other way too. Let's say that instead of BMW deciding not to make silver cars anymore when your car is being driven onto the lot, another car crashes into it. Now your silver BMW has a small dent on the rear bumper with some scratches. As a result, the car has immediately declined in value. But if you want the car, since you've agreed to the options contract, you must pay $67,500, even though with the dent it's only really worth $55,000. You can walk away and lose your $3,000 or pay what is now a premium price on a damaged car.

Another example that is commonly used to explain options contracts is the purchase of a home to be built by a developer under the agreement that certain conditions are met. The buyer will be required to put a non-refundable down payment or deposit on the home. Let's say that the developer agrees to build them the home for $300,000 provided that a new school is built within 5 miles of the development within one year. So, the contract expires within a year. At any time during the year, the buyer has the option to go forward with the construction of the home for $300,000 if the school is built. The developer has agreed to the price no matter what. So if the housing market in general and the construction of the school, in particular, drive up demand for housing in the area, and the developer is selling new homes that are now priced at $500,000, he has to sell this home for $300,000 because that was the price agreed to when the contract was signed. The home buyer got what they wanted, being within 5 miles of the new school with the home price fixed at $300,000. The developer was assured of the sale but missed out on the unknown, which was the skyrocketing price that occurred as a result of increased demand. On the other hand, if the school isn't built and the buyers don't exercise their option to buy the house before the contract expires at one year, the developer can pocket the $20,000 cash.

What is an options contract on the stock market?

An options contract on the stock market is somewhat analogous to the fictitious situation we just described with the car. In the case of the car, we saw that unforeseen events can make the bet made by the buyer and the car dealer profitable or not. The same thing happens in the stock market. Of course in the case of the car, the buyer is simply hoping to get the car they want at what they perceive to be a bargain price, although if BMW really stopped making silver cars, they might sell it to a third party and then get a white one from the dealer. However, in most cases, the buyer wants the car. That isn't the case when it comes to options with stocks.

On the stock market, we are betting on the future price itself, and the shares of stock will be bought or sold at a profit if things work out. The key point is the buyer of the options contract is not hoping to acquire the shares and hold them for a long time period like a traditional investor. Instead, you're hoping to make a bet on the price of the stock, secure that price, and then be able to trade the shares on that price no matter what happens on the actual markets. We will illustrate this with an example.

CALL Options

A call is a type of option contract that provides the option to purchase an asset at the agreed upon amount at the designated time or deadline. The reason you would do this is if you felt that the price of a given stock would increase in price over the specified time period. Let's illustrate with an example.

Suppose that Acme Communications makes cutting edge smartphones. The rumors are that they will announce a new smartphone in the next three weeks that is going to take the market by storm, with customers lined out the door to make preorders.

The current price that Acme Communications is trading at is $44.25 a share. The current pricing of an asset is termed as the *spot price*. Put another way, the spot price is the actual amount that you would be paying for the shares as you would buy it from the stock market right now.

Nobody really knows if the stock price will go up when the announcement is made, or if the announcement will even be made. But you've done your research and are reasonably confident these events will take place. You also have to estimate how much the shares will go up and based on your research you think it's going to shoot up to $65 a share by the end of the month.

You enter into an options contract for 100 shares at $1 per share. You pay this fee to the brokerage that is writing the options contract. In total, for 100 shares you pay $100.

The price that is paid for an options contract is $100. This price is called the *premium.*

You don't get the premium back. It's a fee that you pay no matter what. If you make a profit, then it's all good. But if your bet is wrong, then you'll lose the premium. For the buyer of an options contract, the premium is their risk.

You'll want to set a price that you think is going to be lower than the level to which the price per share will rise. The price that you agree to is called the *strike price.* For this contract, you set your strike price at $50.

Remember, exercising your right to buy the shares is optional. You'll only buy the shares if the price goes high enough that you'll make a profit on the trade. If the shares never go above $50, say they reach $48, you are not obligated to buy them. And why would you? As part of the contract deal, you'd be required to buy them at $50.

We'll say that the contract is entered on the 1st of August, and the deadline is the third Friday in August. If the price goes higher than your strike price during that time, you can exercise your option.

Let's say that as the deadline approaches, things go basically as you planned. Acme Communications announces its new phone, and the stock starts climbing.

The stock price on the actual market (the spot price) goes up to $60.

Now the seller is required to sell you the shares at $50 a share. You buy the shares, and then you can immediately dispose of these at a quality or optimal amount, or $60 a share. You make a profit of $10 a share, not taking into account any commissions or fees.

The Call Seller

The call seller who enters into the options contract with the buyer is obligated to sell the shares to the buyer of the options contract at the strike price. If the contract sets the strike price at $50 a share for 100 shares, the seller must sell the stock at that price even if the market price goes up to any higher price, such as $70 a share. The call seller keeps the premium. So, if the buyer doesn't exercise their option, the call seller still gets the money from the premium.

Derivative Contracts

You probably heard about derivatives or derivative contracts during the 2008 financial crisis. While they can be designed in complex ways, the concept of a derivative contract is pretty simple. What this means is that the contract is based on some underlying asset. For an options contract, the asset is the stock that you agree to buy or sell. The contracts themselves can and are bought and sold. That is why you may have heard about people trading in derivatives. The stock that is the subject of an options contract is called the *underlying*.

So, if you buy an options contract using the Apple stock price as a basis, the term "underlying" would be applicable to the stock from Apple.

Profits from the Call

Keep in mind the brokerage may have some additional fees. However, using our numbers remember that we paid a premium of $1 per share, and the strike price was $50. Computing for profit is one of the basics when it comes to trading. It is where profits are determined and forecasted for future options to buy or sell.

The profit per share was:

Profit = $60 − ($50 + $1) = $9 per share

The contract was for 100 shares, so the total profit would be $90.

What happens if the strike price isn't reached?

The strike price is the fundamental piece of information you need to keep in mind when trading options. If the strike price isn't reached, then the option will simply expire and be worthless. The difference between the current market price or spot price and the strike price is a measure of the profit per share that you will make.

For example, $100 is the price of the stock, and the strike price is $75, then the profit (disregarding fees) will be $25. If the strike price was $95, then the profit per share would only be $5. While the pay off from a strike price that is closer to the actual market price is smaller, it's more likely to pay off than a strike price that predicts a big move.

Why purchase a call option

The reason that you purchase an options contract is to reduce your risk. When you buy an options contract, the only money you're putting at risk is the premium. In the case of our hypothetical example, that is $100. If the stock doesn't surpass the strike price, you can simply walk away from the deal and only lose the $100.

You could, of course, buy the stocks outright and hope to profit. To buy 100 shares, you'll have to invest substantially more money:

100 x $44.25 = $4,425.

If the stock goes up value, then you'll make some money. However, suppose that your hunch about the markets was wrong. Maybe Acme Communications, rather than announcing a new phone that will be in high demand, instead reveals that their next phone will be delayed for a year.

If you decide to unload the stocks you bought for $4,425, you will only get $4,000, and you'll have lost $425.

On the other hand, you can see how you reduced your risk by purchasing a call option. In that case, you won't exercise your right to buy the stock and only lose the premium. Your total loss would be $100.

The Flexibility of Options

In normal stock trading, you're betting on one direction, that the value of the stock will go up with time. And you're battling the opposite, hoping to avoid losses if the stock declines.

Options open the door to making a profit when stocks decline in value. Of course, it depends on being able to make the right call, but if you bet on a stock losing value and you're right, you can make substantial profits. Timing and the size of your trade will be important too, and you'll have to stay focused on the strike price and the current market price of the underlying.

Put Options

A call option is the option to buy a stock if it reaches the strike price. Now let's look at the opposite situation. A *put* is an option contract where you get the right but not the obligation to *sell* a stock before the contract expires. Returning to our previous example, suppose that Acme Communications looks to be heading to bad times and the stock is trading at $44.25 a share. Your bet is that it's going to decrease to at least $35 a share, so you buy a put option with a strike price of $35 a share. If your bet that the stock will decline in value and you're correct, let's say it drops to $30 a share, then you can make a $5 per share profit on the sale. If the stock meets the strike price, the seller of the put is obligated to purchase the stock at that price. In other words, even though the stock has dropped in value to $30 a share on the market, they must buy the shares from you at $35 a share.

Let's suppose that instead it only drops to $38 a share. In this case, you don't have to sell and simply walk away from the deal having paid the premium. So once again, as was the case with a call option, the premium is really the only money that you risk as to the buyer.

The seller of a put option *must* buy the stock from you at the strike price if you exercise your option. If the strike price is $35 but for some reason, the stock crashes to $1, the seller of the put must buy the shares from you at $35.

Why Buy a Put Option?

The answer is simple – when you buy stocks the usual way, you don't make any money from the declining values of stocks. You lose money. With a put option, it gives you the possibility of betting on the stock losing value.

Summary: Buyers of Options

The buyer of an options contract:

- Must pay the premium. This is non-refundable, so the premium is the minimum amount of capital you invest and is the amount you risk.

- You are not obligated to buy or sell any stock even when the deadline arrives.

- You have purchased the right to buy or sell the stock.

- If you buy a call, then you have the option to purchase the expiry of the agreement. If you buy a put, you have the option to sell the stock when the expiry arrives. The option to sell only falls in instances when there is a marked difference between the market price and your own strike price; with the market price being too low.

Summary: Sellers of Calls and Puts

Later we'll see that you may want to sell options and there are good reasons for doing so. Right now, we'll just summarize the general principles.

- The seller of an options contract will keep the premium no matter what. So, if the buyer doesn't exercise their option, you keep the premium as profit.

- If the buyer of a call option exercises their option to buy the stock, you must sell it to them at the strike price. So, if the strike price is $40 but the current market price is $65, you are missing out on a large profit per share. However, as we'll see later this can still be profitable.

- If the buyer exercises their right on a put contract, you must buy the stock from them at the deadline.

Number of Shares

The number of shares in one options contract is 100 shares. Typically, traders will trade multiple contracts. To you'll get the profit per share and then calculate total profit as (profit per share * 100 shares * # of contracts).

Now let's get familiar with the industry jargon so you can have a better understanding of what is going on when you start trading.

Chapter 5 How Options Prices are Determined

Options prices are determined in part by the price of the underlying stock. But options prices are also influenced by the time left to expiration and some other factors. We are going to go over all the different ways that the price of a given option can change and what will be behind the changes. It's important to have a firm grasp of these concepts so that you don't go into options as a naïve beginning trader.

Market price of shares

The largest factor that impacts the price of an option is the price of the investment known as the stock that is behind the option. However, it's not a 1-1 relationship. The amount of influence from the underlying stock is going to change with time. Furthermore, it depends on whether the option is in the money, at the money, or out of the money. The fraction of the options price that is due to the price of the underlying stock is called the options *intrinsic value.*

If an option can be exactly the same as the market pricing or not be comparatively favored, it has zero intrinsic value. An option would have to be priced in the money in order to have any intrinsic value.

- For a call option, if the market price is lower than the strike price or the same, the option will have no pricing at all from the intrinsic value. If the share price is higher than the price used to trade shares via the option, the option will have intrinsic value.

- For a put option, if the share price is at or above the strike price, the option will have zero intrinsic value. If the share price is below the strike price, then the option will have some value from the stock. This is called intrinsic value.

However, to confuse matters, even when an option is at or out of the money, the price of the underlying stock has some influence that can change the value of the option. The amount of influence that the market price of the item known as the stock has on the price of the option is given by a quantity that is called *delta*. You can read the value for delta by looking at the data for any option that you are interested in trading. It is given as a decimal value ranging from 0 to 1 for call options, and it's given as a negative value for put options. The reason it's given as a negative value for put options is that this reflects the fact that if the stock price is found to increase, the price of a put option will be reduced. In contrast, if the stock price declines, the value of the put option will increase. It's an inverse relationship, and thus, the delta is negative for put options.

To understand how this will play out, let's look at a specific example. Suppose that we have a $100 option. That is, the strike price is set to $100. If the price of the underlying stock is $105, delta for the call option is 0.77.

That means that if the dollar value of the stock increases by $1, the value of the option will rise by approximately 77 cents. This is a per-share price change. So, for the option that you are trading, there are 100 underlying shares. So, a 77 cent price rise would actually increase the value of the option by $77.

For a put option with the same strike price, the option would be out of the money, because the share price is higher than the strike price. In this case, for the put option, the delta is given as -0.23. That means that the put option would lose approximately $23 if the share price went up by $1. On the other hand, if the share price dropped by $1, the put option would gain $23.

The intrinsic value of the call option described in this theoretical exercise would be $5 per share. The total cost of the option would be $6.06 per share, reflecting the fact that the call option has $1.06 in extrinsic value. In contrast, the put option has zero intrinsic value. It has almost the same extrinsic value, however, at $1.03.

I have used a 45-day time frame prior to expiration for this exercise. Options prices are actually governed by mathematical formulas, so it's possible to make estimates of what the option price is going to be ahead of time. There are many calculators and spreadsheets that are available free online for this purpose.

Now, let's say that instead, the share price was $95 so that the call option was out of the money and the put option was in the money. In this case, the call option has zero intrinsic value, and it has a $0.94 extrinsic value, so the option would be worth $94. Delta has switched, but not exactly. In this case, for the call option, the delta is 0.25. If the share price rose to $96, with everything else unchanged, the price of the call option would rise to $1.21 per share. This illustrates that you can still earn profits from cheaper out of the money options.

If the share price stayed at $95, the put option would have a delta of -0.75. Notice that if we take the absolute value and add the delta for the call and the put option, they sum up to 1.0.

So, if you see an option of the call type that has a strike that is lower than the market price, with a delta given by say 0.8, that means the put option with the same strike price and expiration date will have a delta of -0.20.

Delta does more than give you the prediction of changes in the underlying share price and price movements of the option. It also gives you a (rough) estimate of the probability to expire in the money for the contract known as an option.

If you sell to open, you don't want the option to expire in the money. Therefore, you are probably going to sell options that have a small delta. On the other hand, if you buy to open, you want the option to go in the money, if it isn't already. So, you would buy an option with a higher delta.

If we say that a given call option has a delta of 0.66, this indicates if we see changes such that the underlying stock price rises by $1, the price of the option on a per-share basis will rise by $0.66. But it also tells us that there is a 66% chance that this option will expire in a positive condition, that is it will be in the money.

Something else you need to know is that delta is dynamic. If the price of a share increases on the market, delta rises for the call option and gets smaller in magnitude for the put option. A declining share price will have the opposite effect.

The amount that delta will change is given by another "greek" – gamma. Most beginning traders probably aren't going to be too worried about gamma, what we've described so far is actually all you need to know to enter into effective options trades. But gamma will tell you the variation in the value of the delta with a change in stock price. So, if gamma is 0.03, this means that a $1 rise in the stock price will increase delta by 0.03 for a call option. The inverse relationship holds for a put option.

If an option is at the money, the delta is going to be about 0.50 for a call option and -0.50 for a put option. That makes sense, if the strike price is equal to the share price on the market, there is a 50% probability that the market price will move below the strike price, and there is a 50% probability that the market cost of shares will move above the strike price.

Implied Volatility

One of the most important characteristics of options after considering delta and time decay is the amount a stock price varies with time. Volatility will give you an idea of how wild the price swings of stock are. If you look at a stock chart, I am sure that you are used to seeing the price go up and down a lot giving a largely jagged curve. The more that it fluctuates, and the bigger the fluctuations in price, the higher the volatility. Of course, everything is relative and so you can't say that any stock has an "absolute" level of volatility. What is done is the volatility for the entire market is calculated, and then the volatility of a stock is compared to the volatility of the market as a whole. When looking at the stocks themselves, this is given by a quantity called beta.

If the stock generally moves with the stock market at large, beta is positive. If beta is 1.0, that means that it has the same volatility as the entire market. That is a stock with average volatility.

If beta is less than 1.0, then the stock doesn't have much volatility. The amount below 1.0 tells you how much less volatile the stock is in comparison to the market as a whole. So, if the beta is given as 0.7, this means that the stock is 30% less volatile than the market average.

If beta is greater than 1.0, then the stock is more volatile than the average. If you see a stock with a beta of 1.42, that means the stock is 42% more volatile than the average for the market.

If beta is negative, that means the stock, on average, moves against the market. When the market goes up, it goes down and vice versa. Most stocks don't have a negative beta but they are not hard to find either.

Volatility is a dynamic quantity, so when you look it up, you are looking at a snapshot of the volatility at that given moment. Of course, under most circumstances, it's not likely to change very much over short time periods like a few weeks or a month. There are exceptions to this, including earnings season.

Implied volatility is a quantity that is given for options. Implied volatility is a measure of the coming volatility that the stock price is expected to see over the lifetime of the option (that is until the expiration date).

One of the things that make options valuable is the probability that the price of the stock will move in a direction that is favorable to the strike price. When an option goes in the money, or deeper in the money (that is the share price moves even higher relative to the strike price of a call, or lower relative to the strike price of a put), the value of the option can increase by a large margin.

If a stock is more volatile, there is more chance of this happening, since the price is going to be going through larger price swings. Therefore, the higher the implied volatility, the higher the price of the option.

In the following, we will consider a hypothetical situation to illustrate. This time, we will look at an option that would have a strike price that was set to a hundred dollars and a $100 share price, so the option is exactly at the money. Here are the prices that you would see for some different values of implied volatility:

- Implied volatility = 40%: Option price is $562.

- Implied volatility = 20%: Option price is $282

- Implied volatility = 10%: Option price is $142

- Implied volatility = 80%: Option price is $1,119

That is for a call option.

As you can see, implied volatility has quite a large influence on the price of an option. For this reason, professional options traders look at implied volatility just as much as they look to the comparison between the strike price and the market stock price. One way to make profits is to seek out options that have high implied volatility.

Each quarter, companies report their earnings. This is one time when implied volatility is going be really important. Earnings calls can send the price of a stock up or down by a large amount. Prices can move $10, $20, or $40 a share in one direction or the other depending on whether the earnings call beat expectations or not, and whether or not there was a piece of good or bad news thrown in with the earnings report. In other words, this is a highly volatile situation.

This offers opportunities for profits. The way that professional traders handle this is they purchase options on companies that are going to have upcoming earnings calls. Typically, you might purchase options about a week ahead of the earnings call. At that time, the implied volatility is going to be relatively low. It may be in the range of 15-20%.

As time passes and it gets closer to the earnings call, implied volatility will go up by a lot. In fact, for the examples above it was no accident that I selected implied volatility of 80%. Recently, I noticed that the implied volatility on some Tesla options shot up to 82%. As the implied volatility goes up, the value of the option increases, providing an opportunity for profits.

Time Decay

The time left until expiration has a large influence on the price of an option. If an option is valued so that it is the same as the share price, or if it is out of the money, time decay is going to have a significant influence over the value of an option at any given time. For an option that can be said to be in the money, the influence of time decay is going to be much less. The closer you get to the expiration date, time value exerts less influence on the overall price of the option. In that case, it's going to be more influenced by implied volatility and the underlying share price. To take an example, at four days to expiration, a $100 strike price on an underlying stock when the market price is set equal to $110 per share will have $10 in intrinsic value with $0.56 in extrinsic value and a total price per share of $10.56. So the price is heavily weighted to the underlying price of the shares. However, theta is -0.23, meaning that on a per-share basis, at market open the following day, the option will lose $0.23 in value, all other things being equal. Of course, all other things are not equal, and changes in share price and implied volatility may wipe that out or add to it.

The important thing to do is check theta every afternoon so you can estimate what the cost is going to be for holding the option overnight. Time decay is an exponential phenomenon, so it decays faster the closer you get to the expiration date. The important path for the trader is knowing when other factors are going to be more important than time decay, you are not simply going to sell off your option because it's going to lose value from time decay the following morning.

Risk-Free Rate

You are also going to see the risk free rate quoted for an option. This is the interest rate that you could earn on an ideal safe investment. Generally speaking, this would be the interest you could earn from a 10-year U.S. treasury over the time period of the option. In normal times, this is an important factor to consider. Rising interest rates (that is significantly rising) can lower the value of options. In recent years, interest rates have been very low, and changes in interest rates have been small and very conservative. So at the present time at least, this is not really something to worry about.

Summary: The Greeks

The Greeks tell us the sensitivity to changes in the factors behind the contract that impact the price of the option.

- Delta: This measures how much the price of the option will vary if there is a single dollar move in the share price, and it also gives the probability that the option contract will come to an end favorably for the buyer. That is it would be in the money.

- Theta: This tells you the amount the price would decline by if a single day has passed. Its impact is felt when the market opens.

- Vega: This measures how responsive the option is if there is an alteration in implied volatility. It tells you how much the price of the option will change in response to a 1% change in the implied volatility.

- Rho: This tells you how responsive the option is to a variation of the risk-free interest rate. It estimates how much the price of the option will change in response to a 1% change in interest rates.

- Gamma: This tells you how much delta will be varying as a result of a change in the underlying stock price.

Before you invest in an option, you should check the values of the greeks. Then determine the relationship of the option strike price. Ask if it is in the money or out of the money, and determine what the implied volatility is.

Volume and Open Interest

Volume and open interest are not going to be factors you consider when trading an option. However, you also need to consider how difficult it's going to be when exiting a position. If you sell to open, as we'll see later, you might need to buy the option back as part of your strategy. If you buy an option, you want to be able to sell it quickly in order to take profits at a level that you're comfortable with.

Some options might look appealing on the surface, but if you can't buy and sell them quickly, they might be more trouble than they are worth. So, you want the trading activity to be taking place at a reasonable level.

Open interest will tell you the number of option contracts that are out there on the market. This is for a single strike price. It would also be for the same expiration date and one type of option. So, if I have a Tesla call option, consider the possibilities. Suppose that there is a strike price of $250 that expires on August 2, I can look at the open interest to see how many of these contracts are on the market. Generally speaking, you want the open interest to be 100 or higher. For some highly traded securities, the open interest can be in the thousands. This is a dynamic quantity, it will change if more traders sell to open. But the rule of thumb is that 100 or higher gives you enough action on that contract that you can buy or sell later without having to wait a terribly long time to close the position. If open interest is really low, you might not find a buyer or seller at all.

Volume is a measure of how many times that option was traded on the current (if the markets are open) or previous trading days.

So, in addition to checking all the factors we've described in this chapter, you'll want to take a look at open interest as well.

Chapter 6 Writing Options and Earned Income

Now we are going to take a look at options from a different angle. Up until this point, our focus has been on buying and then trading options on the market. But there is another way to make money using options if you are somebody who owns shares of stock. And as we will discover, it turns out you don't need to actually own the shares of stock in order to make some money. Although, you will want to keep in mind that some of the possibilities we are going to examine are riskier than others.

If you recall, when you buy an option, you pay a *premium* for it. Now, you have good chances that when you buy an option during your regular trading, you are probably buying it from somebody who bought it from somebody else and so on. But at some point, someone sold to open the option. So, whoever purchased it, from the writer of the option, paid them the premium, which the seller could use as their own income. Selling options can be a nice way to make a good monthly income.

There are a couple of different ways that you can go about doing this. The first way is to actually own the shares of stock that you use as collateral to cover the option. Remember that there is a chance that an option might be exercised. So that possibility is always there. And if you don't own the shares of stock or have money to cover a purchase, it could be a real problem.

Certain people sell options that then they don't even own the underlying stock for, or have the financial backing to purchase shares, and these are called *naked calls* and *naked puts*.

When it comes to selling options, you have to think not only about whether it is a call option or a put, but you also have to consider whether or not it is covered or naked. Either way, the primary goal in most cases is to make income via monthly or weekly payments from selling options. Let's get started by looking at the simplest case, which is a covered call.

Covered Calls

A covered call works in the following way. The seller of the covered call owns at least 100 shares of the underlying stock. People may be speculating that the price of the stock is going to go up. But you can always take a chance if you think that the stock is not going to go up as much as somebody who is trading options is hoping it will go up. Although the price of an *out of the money* call is not going to be the best price that you could get for an option, the fact that it is out of the money cuts the risk that you will lose your shares if someone exercises the option. Secondly, time decay will work in your favor, since as time passes, if the option remains out of the money, it becomes worthless to the buyer. This might seem a bit confusing at first, so let me give you an example.

Suppose that there is a stock that is trading at $100 dollars a share. Consider selling a slightly out of the money call using shares that are already owned to cover it. In this case, we could choose a strike price that is a little bit higher than the market price for the stock right now. For this example, I will choose a $102 strike price with a 30-day expiration date. The price of the option is $2.57. So, if we had 100 shares, we could make $257 by selling the option. If you had 1,000 shares, you could sell 10 options contracts and make $2,570.

But remember there are risks involved in any financial transaction. In this case, the risk is actually fairly low. It is possible that the price of the stock will rise and go above $102, over a 30-day period. And it is also possible that somebody will choose to exercise their option to buy the shares if that happens. Even if they don't, if it goes in the money, the broker can still exercise the option.

Of course, most of the time, stock prices don't fluctuate all that much. But let's say that the price rose to $103. In this situation, it is possible, although certainly not guaranteed, that somebody might exercise the option. If they did so, you would have to sell your shares at $102 per share. But you can buy an option back if necessary as a way to get out of that kind of trouble.

The stock was trading at $100 dollars per share when you wrote the option, so really you are selling the stock at a higher price, and this is not that big of a deal. You are missing out on the $1 higher price that you could have sold the stock at, had you not written the options contract.

However, you sold the option for $2.57. Then you sell the shares for $102, which is a gain of $2 per share. Now add on the $2.57 per share that you got from selling the options contract, and we are up to $4.57 in earnings per share. So, although you lose a theoretical dollar, had you sold the stock on the open market, which brings us down to $3.57, you still made a profit. Of course, we are not taking into account commissions, but overall that won't have that much impact.

When it comes down to it, the actual risk involved is not really selling the stock. Yes, you are giving up a little bit of upside, but you are also still earning money. The real risk is getting in a situation where you are forced to sell shares of stock that you don't really want to sell.

In fact, that is how these options got their name as "calls." The old lingo was that your shares could be "called away" if somebody decided to exercise the option. That is why they are known as *calls*.

In addition to the risk that you might be giving up a future upside, there are other things to consider. If the stock pays dividends, there could be a risk involving the dividend. In simple words, if it is a dividend-paying stock, you have to keep track of the *ex-dividend date*. This is so that you don't get into a situation where somebody exercises their option to buy the shares, and you have to let go of the shares while also giving the buyer the dividend. So, you are probably going to want to look at the ex-dividend date and wait until that date has passed before selling to open against your shares.

Now, in the event that the stock price stays about the same or even declines, then you are in a situation where there is no risk at all. So, using our example if the stock dropped to $99 dollars a share, or even stayed about $100 a share, the option would end up expiring worthless. In that case, you keep the money you earned from the premium, and then you also keep the shares. So, if you are hoping to keep the shares for a long-term investment, then you are all good. You can then repeat the process and earn more premium by writing more options contracts based on the stock.

Some of the things that we can say about this strategy is that it is not the kind of trade that is going to cause you to lose your life savings. The worst thing that could happen is that you may have to sell the shares of stock and miss out on the little bit of profit that you could have made, should the price of the share boost way beyond the strike price. But you are still going to come out ahead financially even though it might not be as good as you could have come out. And you will have to figure out something else to do with the money once you have the shares called away. It is all money that can be reinvested.

Since the risk is relatively low for this type of transaction, brokerages allow level one traders to sell covered calls. For those of you who don't own 100 shares of any stock, unfortunately, that won't be an option for you. But if you do own some shares and you are willing to take some risk in losing the shares, then this could be a way to generate some monthly income.

Some people sell options that expire in as little time as a week because that can minimize the risk a little bit. The reason is that it has less time for the stock to go beyond the strike price and with only a week left on the option, the extrinsic for time value is decaying rapidly.

There are some other possibilities. You can do what is called a close-out. This means that you purchase the call options back, and as a result, your position is closed out. In this case, you might gain or lose money, depending on what the price of the option is at the time you buy it back. But doing this will allow you to retain your ownership of the stock. If the option is still out of the money, it will be much cheaper than you sold it for, so this won't eat into your profits very much.

There is also the possibility of doing what is called a rollout. So, what you do in this case is you buy back the covered calls and then you sell new ones that have the same strike price, but a longer expiration date. So, if you sold covered calls that expired on May 31st, when getting a rollout you would buy them back before they expire and then sell new ones with the same strike price that expired for example on June 30th.

Roll out and up means that you do the rollout strategy, but instead of keeping the strike price the same, you sell the new options with a higher strike price. Conversely, roll out and down is when you use the rollout strategy, but you sell with a lower strike price.

For people who are not too risk-averse, there is also another possibility that of selling call options with a strike price which is actually below the trading share price. Now, why would you want to take that risk? Because the options sell for a much higher price. Let's look at a quick example.

Suppose that your stock is trading at $100 a share. You could sell a call option that expired in 30 days with the strike price of $90 for $10.45 a share. So that would get you a pretty nice premium payment of around $1000 for every options contract that you sold. However, the problem is somebody could exercise their right to exercise the option. That is because the $90 strike price is going to make that pretty attractive when the stock is trading at a hundred dollars a share. So, the risk is real and higher than it would be had you sold a slightly out of the money option. But maybe you are willing to take that risk. For comparison, if you sold it with a $103 strike price, the option would only sell for $2.19, which is definitely less money.

Naked Call

The next strategy is called a "naked" call. This means that you open a position by selling a call that is not backed by the underlying stock. This is a very high-risk move, but it could also be extremely profitable. To sell naked calls, you are going to have to be a higher-level trader, and you are also probably going to be required to have cash in your account because you might need to buy the shares. The risk is that if the option goes in the money and it's exercised, you will have to buy high and sell low.

Suppose that you sell a naked call with an amount of $101 when the stock is trading at $100. Suppose that the company announces they invented a cure for cancer, and the shares jump to $200 a share. In that case, the risk that the option is going to be exercised is going to be pretty high, since a trader could buy the shares from you at $101 a share, which is $99 less than the market price. So, you would be forced to buy the shares at $200 on the market since you did not own them and then sell them to the buyer of the option at $101 a share. An option contract forces the seller to dispose of the shares by selling at the strike amount with no other considerations. So, if you sold one naked options contract in this scenario you lose $99 a share on 100 shares for a total loss of $9,900.

Of course, you will have to weigh everything when deciding whether or not it is worth taking the risk, in most cases, stocks are not going to fluctuate in price as much as we have described here, especially over the limited time periods of most options. So that means there are good chances of you selling naked calls and earning profits from the premiums without much risk of having the option exercised. But it could happen, and you could definitely lose a lot of money.

Most junior traders do not have a high enough level designation to execute this kind of trade, and you will need a large amount of money in your account or use margin. Losses, in theory, could be infinite. So, the "textbook" level of potential losses for this type of strategy, should the stock go up, could grow without limit, but, of course, in the real world they would be capped.

Naked Puts

One of the most popular ways to sell options for income streams is to sell *naked puts*. There are some risks in this strategy, and you have to have a higher-level designation from your brokerage.

First, let's review what a put option entail. A put option gives the buyer the right, should they choose to exercise it, to sell 100 shares of the underlying stock at the strike price. They would use this strategy to make profits if the share price were to tank.

Consider an example. If the strike price of a put option was $50, and the share price dropped to $25, they could purchase the shares for $25 on the market, and then sell them to the writer of the put option at $50 a share. That would earn a $25 profit per share for the buyer. The only hope for the seller of the option is that the stock price rises again to make up the difference so that they can exit the position. Otherwise, they will suffer a huge loss.

However, there are strategies to protect yourself. When you sell options, you have the right to buy them back. So, if you sell a naked put and the stock starts tanking, you can limit your losses by buying them back.

Let's take a specific example. The share price is trading at $100 a share, and you write a naked put with a strike price of $103 with a 30-day expiry. The put is $5.17, so you earn a premium of $517. Let's say at 20 days to expiration, the price of the stock drops to $60 a share. The put option could be exercised, meaning that the option contract owner could buy the shares at $60, while you would be forced to buy them at the strike price, which was $103 a share. This is another example of big losses.

But you could have used a stop-loss order to mitigate your losses. Use the share price to determine your stop-loss order. We could use $95 as an example and suppose the declining stock hit this price with 24 days to expiration. In that case, the option would be $8.56, so we would be losing $3.39 a share. Buying back the options means that we don't have to buy the shares of stock. The $3.39 (per share) loss we have from buying back the options is painful to be sure, but it is still a lot better than having to come up with the money to buy 100 shares at $103 a share when they are only worth $60 a share on the market.

Please note that to sell naked options you must have a margin account, one with enough cash to cover the option as determined by a formula your broker uses. It depends on the price of the stock and the difference between the strike price and the share price. The amount, obviously, is way lower than what you would need to actually cover for the entire option.

Times when naked strategies could work

If the stock price is dropping it is the right time to write naked calls. In a market where stock prices are dropping, the odds are high that any call options written against the stock are going to expire worthlessly. Your profits from the premiums will be smaller, but the risk is also lower.

If the stock price is rising, instead, it is the right opportunity to write naked puts. The risk of the options being exercised in that case is reduced since it's far less likely that the share amount will go below the strike amount.

Besides, options sold out of the money always succeed in raising income without much risk. The trick is selling them far enough out of the money so that your risk is low. This strategy is routinely used by options traders to earn money via naked puts. If the share price starts getting close to your strike price you buy the option back to avoid getting assigned.

Chapter 7 Options Greeks

Now that we know what influences the prices of options, we are going to make that more quantifiable. This is done using the so-called "Greeks," which are five parameters denoted by Greek symbols (or letters) that quantify the way the price of an option will change. You don't have to know how they work precisely, only what they mean. At any given time, you can look them up to get their values. We start by looking at intrinsic value, that is, how the price of the option changes or varies with the underlying stock's price.

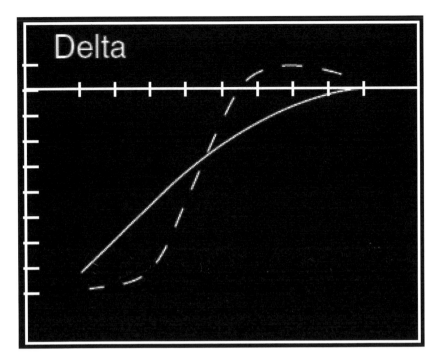

Delta

If you look at the data for any option, you are going to see five Greek letters (usually expressed by their English spelled names) delta, theta, gamma, vega, and rho. The first of these is delta, which tells you how the price of an option changes with the price of the underlying stock.

We noted earlier that the price of an option doesn't have a 1-1 change in price in relation to the stock. You can see exactly how it will change by looking at delta. First, we'll consider call options. So if delta is 0.46, that means if the underlying stock price rises by $1, the price of the option is going to increase by $0.46. If delta was 0.74, then the price of the option would rise by $0.74 if the price of the underlying stock went up by $1.

Put options have a negative delta, which just indicates that a put option has an inverse relationship to the price of the underlying stock. That is if the price of the underlying stock goes down, the value of a put option goes up, and if the price of the underlying stock goes up, the value of the put option goes down.

So if delta is -0.26, and the price of the underlying stock went up by $1, the value of the put option would drop by 26 cents. On the other hand, if the price of the underlying stock had dropped by $1, then the price of the put option would rise by $0.26.

Delta is dynamic, and the number always changes when some important parameter in the options price changes. Consider an option on a stock that is trading at $102 with a strike price of $100, with 14 days to option expiration. In this case, the price of the call option is $2.48, and delta is 0.75. The price of the put option is $0.47, and delta for the put option is -0.25. So if the price of the underlying stock goes up by $1, we expect the call option to rise to $2.48 + $0.75 = $3.23. The price of the put option would decrease to $0.47 - $0.25 = $0.22.

That's just about what happens, but in reality, the relationship isn't quite exact since other things impact the price of the options. The call option increases to $3.84, and the put option declines in price to $0.27.

We said its dynamic, and what happens when the share price rises by $1, is the delta values for both options change as well. Now delta is 0.84 for the call, and -0.16 for the put.

That tells us something important, namely that delta is higher the more in the money the stock is. We can see this looking at some real options. Considering an IBM $124 call that expires on 6/28, it has a delta of 0.967. A $139 call that expires on 6/28 has a delta of 0.5388. The share price is $139.20, so the $124 call is more in the money. The $139 call is practically at the money, and we learn a second important fact about delta, that is that at the money options will have a delta that is reasonably close to 0.50.

Since the more in the money you are, the higher delta, that means in the money options can benefit (or be hurt by) a $1 change in the price of the underlying stock.

Something else that happens is that if the option is in the money, the closer you get to expiration, the higher delta goes. For our example of an option with a $100 share price, if the underlying stock price remains at $103, moving to 7 days from expiration, delta jumps to 0.92 for the call. Moving to 3 days to expiration, delta is 0.98. So if you are expecting a stock price to move a lot in the next few days, getting an option that will expire soon before the move happens could be a worthwhile investment. Look for events that could impact the price, such as an earnings call or product announcement.

Remember at the money options have a delta of about 0.50, and when you get close to expiration, delta for a call will be exactly 0.50, and for a put, it will be -0.5, if the option was at the money. Actually buying at the money options can be quite difficult, so you'll probably have to settle for something close.

If an option is out of the money, the closer to the expiration date, you get the smaller delta gets. In fact, a few days away from expiration delta can get vanishingly small. An out of the money call option for a strike price of $100, share price of $97 with three days to expiration will have a delta of 0.02.

The delta for the same put option will add up the difference to 100 (but remember it's expressed as a negative value). In this case, a put option with the same parameters, so a strike price of $100 – will have a delta of -0.98 if the underlying price is $97. In that case, the put would be worth $3.00, and if the underlying share price dropped to $96, the price of the put would rise to $4. Then you'd see delta increase to -1.00 for the put and drop to 0.00 for the call.

If the stock had moved the other way, risen in price by $1, then delta for the put would drop to -0.92 instead, and the price of the put would drop to $2.04.

The bottom line is delta will give you a good estimate of how much the price of the option will change when the price of the underlying stock changes by $1. If it's a call option, the relationship is direct, and delta is expressed as a positive number. For put options, since the relationship is an inverse one, delta is a negative number. And remember that if you take the absolute value of delta for the put option and add it to the delta value for a call option that has the same strike value and date of expiration, they will sum to 1.0.

Gamma

Gamma is like the second derivative. In other words, it tells you how delta itself changes. This is important since we noted that delta was dynamic. However, beginning traders don't need to dive into this too deeply, but you can check gamma to see about how much delta will change if there is a $1 change in the price of the underlying shares. Gamma has the same value for both puts and calls. So if Gamma were 0.22 and delta was 0.24 for a call option, and -0.76 for a put option with the same strike and expiration date, we'd expect a $1 rise in share price to cause delta for the call option to increase to 0.46, and the delta for the put option would change to -0.54. That is about what would happen, but remember if the option was at the money the values of delta would move to 0.5 and -0.5, respectively.

Theta

When examining options, theta is a very important parameter among the Greeks. What theta gives you information about is the time decay of the option. Theta is expressed as a negative number, reflecting the fact that time decay causes a decrease in option price as time goes on. Let's consider a couple of examples.

Suppose that we have call and put options with a strike price of $100 with three days to expiration. The price of the call is $1.20, and the price of the put is $0.20 if the share price of the underlying stock is $101. In this case, theta is -0.073 for both the call and the put. That tells us that if nothing else changes, the price of each option will decrease by $0.073. The call option is priced at $1.20, and the put is priced at $0.20. Moving to 2 days to expiration and leaving everything else the same, we find that the price of the call option drops to $1.12, and the price of the put option drops to $0.12, so it moved in almost exact accordance to what was expected. The following day theta has increased to -0.079, reflecting the fact that time decay happens more rapidly the closer you get to the expiration date of the option.

In fact, with everything else unchanged, 20 days to expiration theta is about half as strong, at -0.035. That reflects one of the fundamental truths of options, that is that time decay happens in an exponential fashion, with time decay happening faster the closer you get to expiration.

One of the things that help make options seem complicated is that all of these variables are interdependent. So at 20 days to expiration, suppose the stock price shot up to $108. In that case, theta decreases to -0.005. So it's only 1/7th of the previous value. It decreases for the put option as well.

Theta is also proportional to share price. So theta is larger if the share price is larger. Consider a stock with a share price of $975, and a strike price of $1,000. In that case, theta is -0.282 for the call option and -0.274 for the put option. That means if a day passes and nothing else changes, the value of the call option (which in this case is $5.15) will drop by about $0.28, and the value of the put option will drop by about $0.27.

The fundamental lesson here is the same as it was previously, that time decay is an important fundamental when it comes to options pricing. Check the Greek theta to get an idea of how the price of the option is going to decay by the following day if all other things are held equal.

Vega

The next Greek that we are going to meet is Vega, which tells us the relationship between the price of the option and the implied volatility. What Vega tells you is how sensitive the option is to changes in the implied volatility. Generally speaking an in the money option is less sensitive to changes in implied volatility, while an out of the money option is more sensitive to changes in implied volatility. Specifically, vega tells you how much the price of the option will change if the implied volatility changes by 1%. Remember that options that have higher implied volatility are worth more money.

Suppose a stock is trading at $500 a share, and the strike price is $490 with 10 days left to expiration and an implied volatility of 23.5%. Vega will be 0.285. A call will be priced at $13.73, and the put with the same parameters would be priced at $3.69. If the implied volatility increased to 24.5%, then the call would be priced at $14.02, and the put would be $3.98. So, in other words, Vega tells you how much the price of the options increases for every 1 point increase in implied volatility. The closer you get to the expiration date, the smaller vega gets.

When you are in long positions, vega is positive, and it's negative for short positions.

Rho

Rho is a measure of the options pricing's sensitivity to a change in the risk-free interest rate. Since interest rates don't change by that much or that often these days, rho isn't paid much attention to. In a radically changing high-interest rate environment such as existed in the late 1970s, rho would be a more important parameter to pay attention to.

Black-Scholes Equation

The Black-Scholes equation is a mathematical model that describes how derivatives like options behave. It incorporates the option as a function of the underlying stock price and time, the volatility of the stock, and the risk-free interest rate. The equation tells us that gamma represents the gain from holding an option. The equation gives us the "riskless" returns where gamma offsets theta decay. The Black-Scholes equation involves some pretty advanced mathematics, and those with the interest and skills can look up references if they are interested in getting a deeper understanding of the equation. It is a partial differential equation that can estimate the future price of an option. Most options traders don't have to know about the Black-Scholes equation, however. You can simply use tools like spreadsheets or online models that people have created to put the equation into practice for you, and you can play with the various inputs to estimate the future price moves of options you are interested in investing in. The model led to a Nobel Prize in economics. One important fact is that the model is set to work with European options that can be utilized only on the expiration date, and it does not work with American options. However, there are many mathematical models that work quite well for American options.

Chapter 8 Differences Among Forex, Stocks and Options

There are different reasons some traders love to use forex instead of the stock market. One of them is the forex leverage.

We will look at the disparities that exist between forex trading and stock trading.

1. Leverage

When it comes to stock trading, you tend to trade with a cap of leverage of two to one. You must have some requirements on the ground before these can be done. It is not every investor than ends up being approved for that margin account, and this is what a trader needs to be leveraged in a typical stock market.

When it comes to forex trading, the entire system is totally different. Before you can trade using leverage, you need to have opened the forex trading account. That's the only requirement that is out there, nothing else. When you open a forex account, you can easily use the leverage feature.

If you are trading in the United States of America, you will be restricted to a leveraging of 50:1 leveraging.

Countries outside of the US are restricted to leverage of about 200:1. It is better when you are outside the US, than in the US.

2. Liquidity differences

When you decide to trade stocks, you end up purchasing the companies' shares that have a cost from a bit of dollars down to even hundreds of dollars. Usually, the price in the market tends to share with demand and supply.

3. Paired trades

When you trade with forex, you are facing another world, unseen in the stock market. Though the currency of a country tends to change, there will always be a great supply of currency that you can trade. What this means is that the main currencies in the world tend to be very liquid.

When you are in forex trading, you will see that the currencies are normally quoted in pairs. They are not quoted alone. This means that you should be interested in the country's economic health that you have decided to trade in. The economic health of the country tends to affect the worth of the currency.

The basic considerations change from one forex market to the next. If you decide to purchase the Intel shares, the main aim is to see if the stock's value will improve. You aren't interested in how the prices of other stocks are.

On the other hand, if you have decided to sell or buy forex, you need to analyze the economies of those countries that are involved in the pairs.

You should find out if the country has better jobs, GDP, as well as political prospects.

To do a successful trade in the Forex market, you will be expected to analyze not only one financial entity, but two.

The forex market tends to show higher level of sensitivity in upcoming economic and political scenarios in many countries.

You should note that the U.S. stock market, unlike many other stock markets is not so sensitive to a lot of foreign matters.

4. Price sensitivity to trade activities

When we look at both markets, we have no choice but to notice that there is varying price sensitivity when it comes to trade activities done.

If a small company that has fewer shares has about ten thousand shares bought from it, it could go a long way to impact the price of the stock. For a big company such as Apple, such n number of shares when bought from it won't affect the stock price.

When you look at forex trades, you will realize that trades of a few hundreds of millions of dollars won't affect the major currency at all. If it affects, it would be minute.

5. Market accessibility

It is easy to access the currency market, unlike its counterpart, the stock market. Though you may be able to trade stocks every second of the day, five days weekly in the twenty first century, it is not easy.

A lot of retail investors end up trading via a United States brokerage that makes use of a single major trading period every day, which spans from 9:30 AM to 4:00 PM. They go ahead to have a minute trading hour past that time, and this period has price and volatility issues, which end up dissuading a lot of retail traders from making use of such time.

Forex trading is different. One can carry out such trading every second of the day because there are a lot of forex exchanges in the world, and they are constantly trading in one time zone or the other.

Forex Trading Vs Options

A trader may believe the United States Dollar will become better when compared to the Euro, and if the results pan out, the person earns.

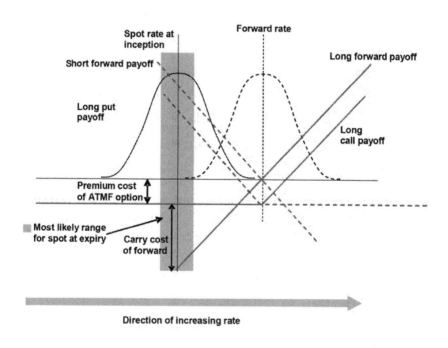

The strategy, if it works, can help in affecting the trade when the research pans out.

When you get involved in Options Trading, you tend to get involved in the purchase and sales of options on great amounts of futures, stocks and so on, that will move either up or below at a price during the phase.

It is similar to Forex Trading, since you can easily leverage the buying power to have a controlling power on futures or stocks.

There exist a number of disparities that exist between Options trading and Forex trading. They are:

1. 24 Hour Trading:

When you get involved in Forex instead of Options trading, you have the capability of trading every second of the day, five days weekly. When you look at the Forex market, you will realize that it lives longer than any financial market in the world.

If you have decided to get double digit gains in the market, it is important to possess a generous amount of time every week to carry out these trades. If a large event occurs anywhere in the world, you may end up being amongst the first to benefit from the situation in the Foreign Exchange market.

You don't expect to spend time waiting and hoping that the market opens in the market like in the case of trading options.

With Forex, you can easily trade anytime you want, at all times of the night and day. Whenever you wish, you can trade it.

2. Rapid Trade Execution:

When you immediately make use of the Forex market; you tend to get instantaneous trade executions. You don't have to be delayed like in the case of Options or some other markets too.

When you place the order, it ends up being filled using the best potential price in the market, instead of wondering what price ends up being ordered.

You won't have to have the urge to slip like the case of options. When you are involved in Foreign Exchange Trading, there is a great chance of liquidity unlike in the case of Options trading.

3. No Commissions:

Forex market is one that doesn't need commission because it acts as an inter-bank market, where buyers are matched with sellers instantly.

There aren't cases of brokerage fees like in the stock market and other markets.

You will see a spread that exists between ask price and the bid, that is the way a lot of Forex trading firms earn their money.

What this means is that when you trade Forex, you stand to save the brokerage fees unlike in the case of options trading, where you are expected to pay communion since you have no choice but to use a brokerage firm.

Forex Trading Risks

Like every financial market out there, there are risks that one may have to face. The interbank market is known to have different degrees of regulations. Apart from that, forex instruments aren't as standardized as other financial market instruments out there. Do you know that in some parts of the globe, there are no regulations to the forex market?

The interbank market consists of different banks all over the world trading with one another.

The banks have no choice but to determine an asset to credit risk and sovereign risks. They have come up with different internal processes, in a bid to ensure that they remain quite safe. These types of regulations are imposed in the industry to ensure that every participating bank is protected.

The market pricing comes from the forces of demand and supply because the market is made up of different banks giving bids and offers.

The fact that there is a great amount of trade flows in the market means that rogue investors can't influence the worth of a currency. This ensures that there is transparency in the foreign exchange market for those traders that are privy to interbank dealing.

A lot of countries have regulations concerning the forex, but not all do.

Pros and Cons of Forex

First Pro:

When it comes to a daily trading volume in every market out there, the forex is the largest, meaning that it possesses the largest amount of liquidity.

This is one reason that one can easily enter or exit a position whenever he wants, for a small spread in a lot of market conditions.

Cons:

Brokers, banks and dealers are known to give a great level of leverage, meaning that investors can easily control huge positions using a tiny amount of money.

Though you don't see it every time, a high ratio of leverage of 100:1 is possible to see in the foreign exchange market. It is important that a trader knows how to use leverage, as well as the risks that using leverage brings to an account. Using a large amount of leverage has forced a lot of dealers to become bankrupt unexpectedly.

Second Pro

You can trade in the foreign exchange market every second of the day, six days in a week. It usually begins daily in Australia and ends in New York.

The main centers for forex are Singapore, Hong Kong, Sydney, Tokyo, New York, London and Paris.

Second Con

Before you can trade currencies in a profitable manner, you have to understand economic indicators and basics. A currency investor has to possess a great understanding of how a lot of economies function, as well as how connected they are. You need to understand these fundamentals that are able to alter the values of currencies.

What Is A Stock

Stock is sometimes called equity or shares. This is a kind of security that shows proportionate ownership when the firm that issues it is concerned. When a person has stocks, he/she is entitled to a proportion of the earnings and assets of the company.

One can buy stocks and sell them on stock exchanges, but this doesn't mean that there aren't other ways of buying and selling stocks. Stocks can also be exchanged in private sales. There is hardly any investor in the financial world that doesn't have stocks in their portfolio.

Before the transactions can be said to be legitimate, they must be in line with the government regulations that have been put in place to shield investors from fraudulent processes.

When compared to a lot of financial instruments, stocks have overshadowed them.

Stock Vs Bond

Companies give out stocks to raise the needed capital to improve their business or get involved in new projects.

Shares can be gotten in different ways. Sometimes, a person may purchase it directly from the firm when it issues it in the primary market. In other cases, the investor may purchase it in the secondary market from another shareholder. Whenever you see a corporation issuing shares, know that it carries it out because it wants to raise money.

Bonds are in another world of its own. Bondholders are seen as creditors to the firm, and they tend to get interest instead of dividends. They are also paid the principal.

When it comes to stakeholders in a company, creditors have more right over the assets and earnings than shareholders when bankruptcy occurs.

The corporation is expected to pay shareholders first before it pays shareholders during a bankruptcy. Shareholders end up being the last in line and may end up getting nothing or a little amount. What this means is that stocks have higher risks than bonds.

If you can't stomach this, you should avoid going for stocks.

What are The Options

Options are those contracts that allow the bearer to be involved in the purchase or sales of a stipulated amount of asset at a fixed price. The bearer has the choice to buy or not, as long as the contract hasn't expired.

Options are bought like a lot of asset classes by making use of brokerage investment accounts.

Options are strong to the extent that they can improve the portfolio of an individual. They can get this done by leverage and added income protection.

Based on the scenarios at hand, different option situations can suit the goals of an investor.

Let's say a stock market is declining; options can be used as an effective hedge to clamp down on downside losses. One can use options to get recurring income. They can also be utilized for speculative purposes like wagering on where the stock price would go.

The way that free lunch doesn't exist in bonds and stocks is the same way that there is no free lunch with options.

There are some risks that one may face when options trading is concerned. You have to understand these risks before you jump into options trading.

This is one reason that when you have decided to trade options with a brokerage company, you are shown a disclaimer that is similar to this:

Options are members of a bigger league of securities, which are called derivatives. The price of a derivative is linked to the price of another thing. Let's make things more transparent. The derivative of a tomato is ketchup. The derivative of grapes is wine. The derivative of a stock is a stock option.

Options can be said to be derivatives of financial securities, meaning that their worth is dependent on another asset's price.

Some examples of derivatives are puts, calls, forwards, futures, and so on.

Call and Put Options

When we say that options are derivative securities, we mean that their price is related to the pricing of another thing. This means that the other thing is what controls the price of the options.

If you purchase the options contract, you are given the right to buy or sell an asset at a stimulate price before the deal expires. You aren't under compulsion to do this.

When a person has a call option, he is given the right to purchase a stock. On the other hand, when a person is given a put option, he has the right to sell the stock.

You can see the call option as a form of down-payment for something that can be gotten in the future.

Let's use a more explicit example. A person sees a new building going up. He may want to have the right to buy it later but says he won't buy it until it has gotten to

108

some stage, or some other condition has been met, this is an example of an option. He can decide to use the option or not. He isn't under compulsion.

Let's say the developer agrees to give the person the right to purchase the house for about a million dollars at any time within the next three years. Before the developer can agree with this, the prospective buyer has to pay a down payment, which can't be refundable. Within that period of three years, the developer isn't allowed to sell the house to anyone else, until after the term expires.

Chapter 9 Options Trading Platforms and Tools

Introduction

Stock options allow people to trade financial securities more specifically stock or equities, bonds, ETFs (Exchange Traded Funds) or mutual funds without making a purchase upfront. A buyer has the option of waiting to see where the price of a particular financial product will fall before making a decision to buy and sell it at a profit. In options trading, you can either purchase a call or put option.

A call option gives you the option of waiting to buy a stock, especially if the trader expects the price to go up.

If the agreed price of a stock was $10 and the price goes up to $12, you buy the stock at $10 and sell it at $12 or hold it. If the price goes down you have no obligation to exercise your option, however, you will have incurred a small premium perceived as a cost for the transaction payable to the seller.

A put option gives the option of buying a stock, especially if the trader anticipated that the stock price would go down. Using the same example if the stock price decreases to $8, you buy the stock at $8 and sell it at $10 thus making a profit. If it goes up, you are only liable for the premium.

Trading Brokers, Platforms and Tools

A person interested in trading options must open an account with a brokerage that offers options. The broker can offer one or several platforms for trading with a wealth of different tools. Each broker or platform has its own pros and cons and it is therefore up to a person to choose which options broker works best of them depending on their expertise, preference, priorities, trading style, and risk appetite.

Some of the best trading brokers, platforms and tools in the market include the following.

1. TD Ameritrade popularly known for their think or swim platform is one of the best brokers for options trading. The broker has won several awards including the Best Overall Online Broker, Best for Day Trading, Best Web Trading Platforms and Best for Beginners. They have many educational videos and content about trading options and their platform has a number of useful tools among them risk management tools. The platform is also popular with professional and expert traders.

2. Interactive Brokers is popular for its low costs. It's trading platform, Trader Workstation has been, for the longest time, the most challenging platform to use; however, they have made continuous efforts to make it simpler so that it can accommodate amateur traders. Their latest tool IBot lets you make inquiries by word of mouth rather than searching through the platform. Their lab also allows potential users to test out their services before making a purchase.

3. As its name suggests, Lightspeed requires traders who are experts and very active. Their platform Livevol X offers expert tools including them, analytical tools not present in other platforms. If you are a beginner at options trading, Lightspeed is not the best broker for you, however, if you are a pro trader the broker has some features you would enjoy.

4. E*TRADE has been in the market as an options trading broker for a long time and caters for both beginners and experts. Some consider this the best overall broker. Its options house platform and Power E*TRADE platform offers a wide variety of tools. One major con is that their commissions are a bit on the upper side.

5. Charles Schwab is another good broker overall. They have a lot of educational material that makes it hard not to succeed in options trading. Their costs are also very competitive. The StreetSmartedge platform has a useful number of tools including those

from optionsXpress, which Schwab purchased by back in 2011.

6. TradeStation is one of the best trading brokers made for expert traders. This is thanks to the fact that the broker used to deal with software for trading. TradeStation has an array of tools including the Options Station tool, which is very useful in analysis. Many of these tools are also available for sale to people using other brokers.

7. Ally Invest is another broker with low costs. They require no minimum account balance or fee meaning that you can trade with almost no money as you learn the game. The expert traders, of course, take advantage of this and continue to enjoy a variety of tools.

How to Open an Options Account

Once you have done your research and reviewed a number of brokerage firms, you can select one broker and open an account with them.

Step 1

The brokerage firm will give you two options; you open either a cash account or a margin account. Cash accounts make use of the money in your account to take care of your trading activities and costs. A margin account, on the other hand, allows you to trade with you financial securities as collateral including options you may have already purchased.

Step 2

After deciding on the account, you will need to deposit a minimum amount of money into your account depending on the broker and type of account you have selected. Most cash accounts do not require a deposit. However, margin accounts require you to put a lease $2,000 as per the federal regulations. Beware of fake trading sites that con people money especially at this stage. Also, make sure that the broker uses safe payment methods.

Step 3

Most brokerage firms will assess your experience and capital investment and give you a trading limit before you engage in trading. This is the case to protect traders from the potential risk associated with online trading. Therefore, a trader must obtain this approval before proceeding.

Step 4

Check out the educational and research content provided by the broker and do your best to understand it before you can begin trading. Even though you might be tempted to assume that the educational content is just basic information that you can do without, please go over everything provided and look for more, because knowledge is power.

Chapter 10 Basic Options Trading Strategies

Once you understand the basics of options trading, you are ready to get the ball rolling. When it comes to options trading strategies, you need to have a trading plan. Your trading plan is what should help you define what kind of strategy you should be used. Based on your trading plan, you can decide to develop a strategy that will cause you to reach your goals.

There is a risk in options trading. However, the most important thing is to know what you are doing. Warren Buffet said, "Risk is where you don't know what you are doing." In trading and investing, there will always be a risk, what you need to understand is to have a clear knowledge about what you are doing. The secret to great and consistent profit in options trading is to develop a good trading plan and then develop a set of strategies that will help you reach them.

When it comes to options trading many people just think of put and call options. Well, that's the start. You need to know the basics of the trade. From there, you want to look at some strategies to enable you to do well in the trading. Based on your trading plan, we will be looking at steps and strategies to ensure you do well in options trading.

Covered Call Strategy

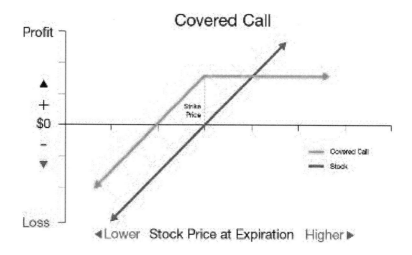

This is one of the strategies that many aspects used to protect their positions in the marketplace while producing income on the options they own. It is the strategy of selling a call option against uncertainty about a stock position. Investors can use this strategy to manage their portfolio when they have a neutral opinion on a stock direction.

To execute a call option, you need to do two things: you have to buy shares of a stock and later sell a call option of the stock you own. However, you need to make sure that you study and analyze the trade winds in the financial market before making this move. Let's consider the case of 100 shares of stock per call option. For every 100 shares of stock you own, you can then sell or write 1 call option against it. In the event that stock increases in price, then the short call will be covered by the long stock position.

You have a long term position on the stock, however, the stock price has increased in value since you bought it. Now, you seem to be feeling neutral about the direction of the call. In this case, through a covered call option, you receive a premium for the sale. But since the stock price has gone up, selling the stock at the strike price with the additional money from the premium allows you to earn much more (strike + premium received) from your position.

Example of Covered Call

If you are looking to earn additional income on the stock portfolio you own, the way to do that is through a covered call. Remember that a call option gives the buyer the right, but not the obligation to buy an underlying stock at a strike price before or at the expiration date. You can use the covered call strategy if you own a stock option that is trending or rising slightly in the financial market.

We are all used to renting a home. Therefore, compare a covered call option for renting a home. You found an agent who is ready to rent a home for you. The real estate agent found the home and you went out to see the home. Everything was good, but you are not ready to move in. To lock the deal, you decided to rent the home with an option to buy.

Before the expiration, you have the right to pay for the rent at the strike price, during the time you paid for the option to rent the home. However, if you fail to exercise the option, you will lose the initial money used to pay for the option to rent the home. This is exactly how covered call options work.

Let's assume that bought 1000 shares of ABC at $ 50 per share, costing $ 5,000. You decided to write ten (10) covered call option against the 1,000 shares of stock you won. Each call option was sold at $ 4, making a total of $ 40. By writing a call option, you are giving the holder the right to buy the underlying stock option at a strike price of $ 50 within or at the expiration date. In exchange for selling the right to own or buy the stock, the buyer of the option pays your premium. What do you do with the premium? You just have to pocket it and deposit into your trading account. If the stock price increase further to $ 80 before the expiration, then the stockholder has lost the premium paid for the contract. Therefore, you still own your stock, but you have earned a profit of 3,400 ($ 40 of premium and $ 3,000 of profit on the increased value of shares).

Steps to Selling Covered Call

One of the important trade strategies taken by many stockholders is selling covered stock options. This strategy is very important because it enables you to earn premiums on stocks while still holding onto the stock until the stock option matures and being exercised by the stock option holder. The following are the basic steps to take if you are looking to sell covered call options.

1. Buy the Stock.

A "covered" call means you first own the underlying stock of a company. Therefore, before you consider selling a covered call, you have to make sure you already have the underlying shares of stock in your brokerage account. Without this, your broker will not allow you to sell the covered via the brokerage account. What are the best strategies to own the stock before placing the call?

• Buy the stock outright: A good way to get the stock of a particular company is to use your online brokerage trading account to place an order. Through the assistance of your broker, you can find stocks of companies in various industries that meet the needs and requirements of your trading plan.

• Find soon to expire "out of money" stock options: Another way to buy the stock option is to simply look for stock options that are soon to expire. Check whether the underlying stock is near to getting "in the money". If that is analysis are right, you can proceed to buy the call option and then pay the value of the strike price to own the underlying shares of stock.

• Find "out of money" stock options: Sometimes, due short time expiration, call stock option of a company will be "out of money". Often times, the trader loses the premium used to buy the call option and then after a few days later the call option gets "in the money". Buying call options of these contract soon after they expire can help you gain access to the underlying stocks.

2. Analyze the stock price movement

Even though you now own the stock, you want to make sure have analyzed the trade and know the current stock market condition. Use your knowledge of technical and fundamental analysis to evaluate the future position of the underlying stock you won. You can decide to study the market, the trend lines and the fundamental news about the underlying company to decide on how the "implied volatility" of the stock will be.

3. Place the Sell Order

After a careful technical and fundamental analysis has been done and you notice the trade winds is likely to blow in your favour, you can then place the order through your brokerage account. Through the help of your online discount broker, you can open and sell the option and earn a premium on the transaction. Through the sale of the premium and the strike price you receive when the call option has been exercised, you stand to make a profit from the trade.

Married Put Strategy

In the auto industry, insurance is very popular. It looks nice and feels good to buy a brand new car, but there are risks associated with the car. Your car can get an accident or simply develop a fault that will cause it to break down. In order to hedge the car against the unknown, you sign up for and vehicle insurance. Every month, you pay a little insurance premium that renews the contract with the insurance company to keep your vehicle intact. Should an accident occurs while driving home or to work, you can just get the insurance company to cover the costs? Why? You have hedged the car against losses.

In stock trading, a married put works like insurance. Just like there unforeseen issues in auto management, there are issues like stock price falling in value. In times of uncertainties, you are looking to protect your stock holding from potential loss in value. So, what do you do? You buy a put option. Remember that a put option gives you the right, but not the obligation to sell the underlying stock at the strike price within a certain date.

A Married Put, also known as Protective Put is a stock option trading strategy used to protect or hedge the value of a stock own by an investor. The Married Put is created when an investor buys shares of a stock and simultaneously purchases put options for the equivalent number of shares owned. The stock and the put are recognized as one and therefore referred to as a "Married Put". This strategy is also known as Synthetic Call because it is a form of mimicking a long call option.

In this case, the protective put option is simply used as a form of insurance of hedge against the underlying stock, adding downward protection to the bullish stock. By purchasing the put option, the holder has the right to sell the stock at the given strike price without having to worry about the falling value of the underlying stock.

A Married Put provides tremendous advantage apart from lowering risk or serving as a form of Insurance if the stock price goes down in value. When you have but a protective put option, you still own the stock and have access to stock ownership benefits such as collecting dividends and voting, unlike having a covered call for an underlying stock. Since each put option has 100 shares, the investor can buy as many contracts to ensure that all the shares of stock have been shielded through the Married Put.

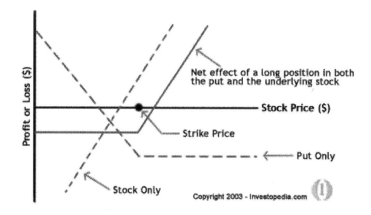

Image: Investopedia (Illustration of Married Put) When you purchase put with a stock, what you lose is the premium, but you are hedging the stock against sharp falls in the market. In the case the stock price falls, you can choose to sell your stock at the strike price of the Married Put, rather than what the stock is currently trading at the market. The put option services as a hedge, to protect you from losing on the value of your stock.

What do you do when the put option is about to expire? If the stock price has fallen below the strike price of the put option (ITM), then it means the put option has served you well. In this case, you can cut your losses in the market by selling the underlying stock to another investor and making a profit. Notwithstanding, if the stock price has is OTM, you can keep the stock and allow it to expire worthless. As the value of the stock progressively increases, you can choose to provide ongoing protection by renewing the put option to hedge it against unexpected losses in the market.

Married Put Example

Let's assume that you bought 100 shares of ABC at $ 80 per share. A total of $ 8,000 was paid for all the shares, excluding brokerage commissions on the transaction. ABC shares seem to be doing well in the stock market. After about three months later, the stock was now trading at a price of $ 120 per share. This is very exciting, seeing the stock price increase in value.

After three months, the value of the stock will be $ 12,000. An unrealized profit of $ 4,000 was made on the purchase of the underlying stock. If you sell the stock at $ 80 per share, you might be leaving a lot of money on the table if the stock price moves to $ 130 a few weeks after. But, you also don't want to lose when the value of the stock goes down. What do you do to solve this dilemma?

You have to buy a put option. A put option gives you the right, but not the obligation to sell the underlying stock at a strike within a period of time. By purchasing a put option for all the 100 shares of stock you won, you are protecting, hedging or securing the stock from losing its value when the trading price of the underlying stock goes down. The put option bought is your insurance.

Therefore, you pay a premium of say, $ 2 for the 100 shares of stock with the right to sell the shares, if you want to, at the strike of $ 120 within the time of the contract. This will cost you $ 200. By buying the put option, you have protected the stock from losing value when the market goes down.

If after a week of buying the put option, the stock price of the underlying just went to $ 90 per share, you can choose to exercise your put option. Instead of selling the stock at a trading price of $ 90, you will have the right to sell the stock option to another trader at a selling price of $ 120 per share. In this case, you stand to make a profit of $ 2,800 (less the cost of the put option), even though the shares of stock has gone down in value. In effect, a put option is a form of insurance of stocks, limiting the amount of money you can lose on the investment, hence protecting you from the downsides of the market.

Collar Options Strategy

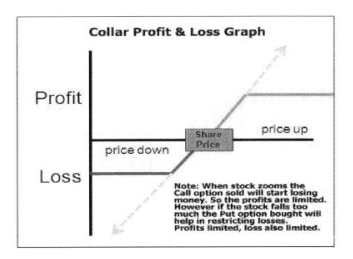

Once you understand how a protective put works, then you want to also look at a Collar Options Strategy. A collar options strategy combines two main options strategies: a protective put and writing a covered call against the shares of stock you already own in your trading account. The protective put limits the loss of your underlying shares and the covered call gives you the opportunity to sell earn unlimited returns on the stock if you believe the underlying stock will go up in value.

Based on your technical or fundamental analysis, you expect you are feeling bullish on a stock you have hedged through a put option. For months, you have hedged your stock through a put option and have profited immensely even though the stock price has decreased in its trading value. However, you noticed that the stock is likely to go in value again. A collar strategy can be used here.

While you can use a collar option to hedge a stock before selling, many experts believe that a collar option is good if you are nearing retirement. Many experts believe that a collar option is not a good strategy for young options traders because if the covered call gets

ITM, the stock option holder can exercise the right and buy the stock at the strike price. Experts believe that young traders are supposed to be daring with their investments.

How Collar Options Work

Collar options work under three main conditions:

• Owning or buying a stock

You can't exercise a collar option if you don't own or buy shares of the underlying stock. This is very important because your broker may not allow you to use a collar option strategy. Therefore, the first thing to do is to buy and own shares of stock. Since there is a part of the covered call in the deal, you will have to own the stock before using this strategy.

It is very important that you buy or own at least 100 shares of stock. Why? Each option contract has 100 shares of stock. If you have less than 50 shares of stock of the underlying stock, you can still not be able to exercise and use this option trading strategy. Therefore, the first step here ensures that you have bought 100 shares of an underlying stock.

• Buying a Put with an "out of money" strike price Once you have at least 100 shares of stock, the next step is to use buy a put option that is out of the money. Notice that a put option gives you the right, but not the obligation to sell the underlying stock at a strike price by expiration. In the case of an "out of money" option, the strike price is below the current stock market. Therefore the stock has been protected from falling in value. This is where a protective put or a married put takes place.

• Writing a covered call at an out-of-the-money strike price

A call option gives the buyer, but not the obligation to buy the stock at or before expiration. If you choose to write a call option after protecting the stock through a put, you will have to make sure that the strike price of the stock option will be higher than the trading price by expiration before you realize a profit.

However, you stand to get a premium when you write the covered call option. One of the reasons some investors prefer writing a call option after buying a put is that they want to use the money generated from the call option to pay for the put option. Should the call

132

option be sold higher than the put option, they may even gain profit from the difference. However, the collar option will be referred to as a "Costless Collar" when the premium generated is just equal to the money used to buy the put option.

Collar Options Strategy Example

This strategy is often used by shareholders after a long position in a stock that has experienced tremendous gains. Shareholders have downside protection (long puts to lock in profits from the falling value of the stock) while writing a covered call to be able to sell shares of the underlying stock at a higher price to realize the profit (selling higher = more profit than at current stock levels).

Let's say you bought 1 00 shares of XYZ, trading at $ 50 per share. The total amount of money paid for the transaction was $ 5,000. You held the stock for almost two years and have participated in dividends. After those two years, the share of stock is now trading at $ 150. That means you have made an unrealized profit of $ 1, 000.00.

Well, at this stage, you can choose to sell the stock and exit the market. But looking at the growth trend of the company, you've noticed that the stock shares has the potential to grow further, even though there is some slight volatility in the market.

Instead of selling the stock to pocket the profit, you decided to use a collar options strategy. Since the underlying stock has begun to fluctuate in price, you decided to hedge the stock against any fall in stock price. The first thing you did to hedge the stock is to buy an "out of money" put option. You paid a premium of $ 1.5 for the protective put options contract at a strike price of $ 150.00. The entire put option contract cost you a total amount of $ 150.00 ($ 1.5 x 100 shares of stock).

Looking at the prospects of the company, you went ahead and then wrote a covered call option at 1.5 per contract and you earned a premium of $ 100 ($ 1.00 x 150 shares) from the sale of the call option. You lost nothing because the price of the call option premium paid for the put option premium. By expiration, you noticed that the stoke price has increased even further to $ 159.00. In this case, you have protected your stock of shares from falling but at the same time made more profit from the increase in the share of stock. On the other hand, if the share price goes down in value, the call option holder will exercise the call and then buy the underlying stock at the strike price of $ 150.00. You will still lose nothing from this transaction, however, you may lose on the future earnings of the stock to the new investor or trader.

Covered calls, protective puts and collar strategy are triplet strategy that you can use to grow your portfolio. However, you need to understand how each works. Once you are experienced with how each them works, then you can combine the three strategies to implement a collar strategy. Always do your analysis and evaluation of the market before using any of these basic trading strategies. Meanwhile, you might to also use some advanced trading strategies to grow your portfolio.

Hedging Vs. Speculation

Hedging and speculation have become one of the hot topics in the area of stock options trading. Many traders seem not to understand the difference between these two investing terminologies and how they apply to grow an asset portfolio. A good understanding of how hedging and speculation works will enable you to see what the ordinary trader does not see.

What's speculation? It is the act of trying to make a profit on a security's price change or volatility in the financial market. Speculation can be done when underlying security, in this case, the stock is highly volatile. A speculator which could be a stock options trader maximizes the benefit of price changes through better analysis of the stock and making more accurate predictions.

The more accurate the prediction and the corresponding strategies used, the more profit that will be earned through the act of speculation. An investor using speculation to make a profit in the financial market is said to be a risk lover. In some trading, the speculator may win while losing some cases. It all depends on analysis, evaluation and using the right trading strategies.

Hedging deals with an attempt to reduce the risk of underlying security due to the fluctuations in the marketplace. Hedging helps in eliminate the volatility and losses associated with an underlying asset. A hedge is considered as a form of insurance on an asset, preventing it from falling in value below the current trading price.

When you hedge a stock from any losses, you are still allowed to vote and partake in dividend sharing. However, the downside of hedging is that the underlying stock is restricted from any gains of the asset. Using a hedge is a very good investment strategy, but you should also look at the downside of not partaking in gains. Generally, investors hedging a stock they own if there is a lot of volatility in the market. They are feeling bearish about the underlying stock and thinking that it might experience a downward movement which will decrease the stock price and also increase the value. This is done by buying put options for protection.

Thus, an investor can purchase one put option to protect against a decrease a share value by buying a small amount of money for the premium. If the stock price falls, the investor will lose money in the long position. However, profits will be made on the put. and shareholders consider

Chapter 11 Financial Leverage

Leverage is a concept that is used by both companies and investors. For investors, the notion of leverage is used to try and increase returns that come on investment. To use leverage, you have to make use of various instruments, including future, options, and margin accounts.

The use of leverage n options trading helps boost your profits. Trading in options can give you huge leverage and allow you to generate huge profits from a small investment.

Definition

Leverage is the ability to trade a large number of options using just a small amount of capital. Many traders feel that leverage is, but studies have found that the risk in leveraged options is nearly the same to non-leveraged securities.

Why Is Leverage Riskier?

Trading options using leverage is usually considered riskier because it exaggerates the potential of the business. For instance, you can use $500 to enter a trade that has a potential of $7000. Remember the first rule of trading – don't trade what you cannot lose.

This isn't as true as it seems, which is why it is vital that you know what you are doing at all times.

Leverage makes you utilize capital more efficiently. For this reason, many traders love the trade because it allows them to go for larger positions with limited capital.

When you use leverage, you don't reduce the potential profit that you will gain; rather, you reduce the risk in certain trades. For instance, if you want to put your money in 10,000 options at $8 per share, you would need to risk $80,000 worth of investment. This means that the whole amount of $80,000 would be at risk.

However, you can use leverage to place a smaller amount of money, thus reducing the risk of loss.

This is the way you need to look at leverage, which is the right way.

Before you can trade leverage, you need to find a way to maximize the gains in each trade. Here are a few tips that you can explore:

Know When to Run

You need to cut losses early enough and then let your winning trades run to completion. Just the way you run other trades; you need to know when to cut your losses so that you don't end up bankrupt. You need to make use of stop losses when running leverage in trades.

Have a Stop Loss Set

As a trader, you need to determine your stop loss set so that you don't lose more than you can afford. The set that you come up with will depend upon the situation of the market at any time. Whatever the case, always make sure you have a set to guide you.

Don't Go With the Trade

Many traders try to chase a trade to the finish, something that ends up discouraging them and making them lose money. Once a move happens, you need to accept and wait for the next opening. Always be patient because just like the other opportunity came *along, another one will definitely come by.*

Have Limit Orders

Instead of placing market limits, opt for limit orders instead so that you can save on fees. The limit orders also help you reign in your emotions when you trade.

Learn About Technical Analysis

Make sure you learn about technical analysis before you jump into trading. Technical analysis will make sure you have the information that you need to make decisions fast.

The Advantages of Leverage in Options Trading

When you use leverage, you increase your financial capability as a trader and enjoy better trading results. You can change the amount of leverage at your discretion. This is because when you open a trading account, you have all the power of managing the amount of capital that you place on a trade. The good news is that you can use leverage free of charge, but you need to make sure you know how it works and whether it will work for you or not.

The level of leverage varies. Some trading platforms offer leverage from as low as 1:1 up to and beyond 1:1000. As a trader, it is advisable that you go for the largest leverage possible so that you can make the biggest returns.

Another advantage is that low leverage allows you as a new trader to survive. When starting out in options trading, you have the capacity to make small trades with little to show for your efforts. With leverage, you can make use of leverage to place trades that run into thousands of dollars without risking the same amount in terms of investment. As long as you know what you are doing, you have the capability to enjoy massive profits.

Disadvantages of Leverage in Options Trading

As much as it is a good way to make huge profits, you also need to understand that leverage comes with many demerits. These include:

Magnifies the Losses

With leverage, you will be faced with huge losses if the trade decides to go the other way. And since the original outlay is way smaller than what you end up losing, many traders forget that they are placing their capital at risk. Make sure you come up with a ratio that will help protect your interests and then know how to manage trade risk.

No Privileges

When you use leverage to trade, you sacrifice full ownership of the asset. For instance, when you use leverage, you give up the opportunity of enjoying dividends. This is because the amount on the dividend is deducted from the account regardless of the position of the trade.

Margin Calls

A margin call is when the lender asks you to add funds so that you keep the trade open. You have to decide whether you wish to add funds or exit a position to reduce the exposure.

Incur Expenses

When you use leverage to trade options, you will receive the money from the lender so that you can use the full position. Most traders opt to keep their positions open overnight, which attracts a fee to cover the costs.

How Much Leverage Do You Need in Options Trading

Knowing how to trade options needs detailed knowledge about the various aspects of economics. For many people, the lack of knowledge to use leverage is the major cause of losses.

Studies show that many traders who opt for options lose money in the process. This happens whether for smaller or high leverage.

Risks of High Leverage

In options trading, the capital for placing a trade is usually sourced from a broker. While you have the ability to borrow huge amounts to place on a trade, you can gain more if the trade is successful.

A few years back, traders were able to offer leverages of up to 400 times the initial capital. However, rules and regulations have been, and at the moment, you can only access 50 times what you have. For instance, if you have $1000, you can control up to $50,000.

Choosing the Right Leverage

You need to look at different factors when choosing the kind of leverage that will work for you.

First, you need to start with low levels of leverage, because the more you borrow, the more you will need to pay back. Second, you need to use stops to make sure you protect the amount you have borrowed. Remember losses won't go down well with you.

All in all, you need to choose leverage which you find is comfortable for you. If you are a beginner, go for low leverage so that you minimize risks. If you know what you are doing, then go for maximum leverage to build your returns.

Using stops on order allows you to reduce loses when the trade changes direction. As a newbie, this is the only protection you need to make it in the market. This is because you will learn about the trades and how to place them while limiting any losses that might arise.

How to Manage Risk in Options Trading

Options trading comes with a number of risks that you need to manage so that you can enjoy the profits and minimize losses.

Here are a few risks and how to deal with them.

Losing More than What You Have

This risk is inherent in options trading, especially if you are using leverage to make a trade. It means that you put up a small fraction of the initial deposit to open the trade. This means that your fate is in the hands of the direction of the market. If it goes along with your prediction, you will gain more than the deposit. On the other hand, if the direction changes and you lose the position, you might end up losing more than your initial deposit.

When this happens, you need to have a strategy in place to help mitigate the risk. What you need to do in this case is to set a limit, so that you define the exact level at which the trade should stop so that you don't lose more than you can handle.

Positions Closing Unexpectedly

When positions close unexpectedly, they lead to loss of money. To keep the trades open, you need to have some money in the account. This aspect is called the margin, and if you don't have enough funds to cover the margin, then the position might close.

To mitigate this, you need to keep an eye on the running balances and always add funds as needed.

Sudden Huge Losses or Gains

The market can turn out to be volatile, and when it does, you need to move fast. Markets change depending on the news or something else in the market, which can be an announcement, event, or changes in trader behavior.

Apart from having stops, you also need to get notifications regarding any upcoming movement, which tells you whether to react or not,

Orders Filled in Erroneously

When you give instructions to a broker to place a trade for you, and the broker instead does the opposite. This is termed slippage. When this happens, use guaranteed stops to make sure you protect yourself against any slippage that might occur.

How to Trade Smarter Using Leverage

Even with leverage in tow, you need to have a way to trade better. With many mistakes occurring during a trade, you stand to lose more than gain if you don't have the right tips to excel. Let us look at the top mistakes that you go through to get to the top.

Misunderstanding Leverage

Many beginners don't understand leverage and go ahead to misuse this feature, barely realizing the risk they are exposing themselves to.

To make this work for you, learn about leverage, and master it. Understand what it is and what it isn't and then find out the best ways to make use of it. You also need to understand how much you can put in without running huge losses.

Having No Exit Plan

Just like socks, you need to control your emotions when trading options. It doesn't mean that you have to swallow your greed and fear; rather, you need to have a plan that you can go with. Once you have a plan, you need to stick to it so that even when things aren't going your way, you have something to guide you to make a recovery.

You need to have an exit plan, which means you know when to drop a trade.

Failure to Try New Strategies

148

You need to make sure you try out a few new strategies depending on the level of trading you want to achieve. Most traders get a single strategy and then stick to it even when it is not working out for them. When this happens, you are often tempted to go against the rules that you set down.

Maintain an open mind so that you can learn new option trading strategies to help you get more out of your trades.

Chapter 12 Covered Calls

In this chapter, we'll investigate a trading strategy that is a good way to get started selling options for beginners. This strategy is called covered calls. By covered, we mean that you've got an asset that you own that covers the potential sale of the underlying stocks. In other words, you already own the shares of stocks. Now, why would you want to write a call option on stocks you already own? The basis of this strategy is that you don't expect the stock price to move very much during the lifetime of the options contract, but you want to generate money over the short term in the form of premiums that you can collect. This can help you generate a short-term income stream; you must structure your calls carefully.

Setting up covered calls is relatively low risk and will help you get familiar with many of the aspects of options trading. While it's probably not going to make you rich overnight, it's a good way to learn the tools of the trade.

Covered Calls involve a long position

In order to create a covered call, you need to own at least 100 shares of stock in one underlying equity.

When you create a call, you're going to be offering potential buyers a chance to buy these shares from you. Of course, the strategy is that you're only going to sell high, but your real goal is to get the income stream from the premium.

The premium is a one-time non-refundable fee. If a buyer purchases your call option and pays you the premium, that money is yours. No matter what happens after that, you've got that cash to keep. In the event that the stock doesn't reach the strike price, the contract will expire, and you can create a new call option on the same underlying shares. Of course, if the stock price does pass the strike price, the buyer of the contract will probably exercise their right to buy the shares. You will still earn money on the trade, but the risk is you're giving up the potential to earn as much money that could have been earned on the trade.

You write a covered call option that has a strike price of $67. Suppose that for some unforeseen reason the shares skyrocket to $90 a share. The buyer of your call option will be able to purchase the shares from you at $67. So, you've gained $2 a share. However, you've missed out on the chance to sell the shares at a profit of $35 a share. Instead, the investor who purchased the call option from you will turn around and sell the shares on the markets for the actual spot price and they will reap the benefits.

However, you really haven't lost anything. You have earned the premium plus sold your shares of stock for a modest profit.

That risk – that the stocks will rise to a price that is much higher than the strike price - always exists, but if you do your homework, you're going to be offering stocks that you don't expect to change much in price over the lifetime of your call. So, suppose instead that the price only rose to $68. The price exceeded the strike price so the buyer may exercise their option. In that case, you are still missing out on some profit that you could have had otherwise, but it's a small amount and we're not taking into account the premium.

In the event that the stock price doesn't exceed the strike price over the length of the contract, then you get to keep the premium and you get to keep the shares. The premium is yours to keep no matter what.

In reality, in most situations, a covered call is going to be a win-win situation for you.

Covered Calls are a Neutral Strategy

A covered call is known as a "neutral" strategy. Investors create covered calls for stocks in their portfolio where they only expect small moves over the lifetime of the contract. Moreover, investors will use covered calls on stocks that they expect to hold for the long term. It's a way to earn money on the stocks during a period in which the investor expects that the stock won't move much at price and so have no earning potential from selling.

An Example of a Covered Call

Let's say that you own 100 shares of Acme Communications. It's currently trading at $40 a share. Over the next several months, nobody is expecting the stock to move very much, but as an investor, you feel Acme Communications has solid long-term growth potential. To make a little bit of money, you sell a call option on Acme Communications with a strike price of $43. Suppose that the premium is $0.78 and that the call option lasts 3 months.

For 100 shares, you'll earn a total premium payment of $0.78 x 100 = $78. No matter what happens, you pocket the $78.

Now let's say that over the next three months the stock drops a bit in price so that it never comes close to the strike price, and at the end of the three-month period, it's trading at $39 a share.

The options contract will expire, and it's worthless. The buyer of the options contract ends up empty-handed. You have a win-win situation. You've earned the extra $78 per 100 shares, and you still own your shares at the end of the contract.

Now let's say that the stock does increase a bit in value. Over time, it jumps up to $42, and then to $42.75, but then drops down to $41.80 by the time the options contract expires. In this scenario, you're finding yourself in a much better position. In this case, the strike price of $43 was never reached, so the buyer of the call option is again left out in the cold. You, on the other hand, keep the premium of $78, and you still get to keep the shares of stock. This time since the shares have increased in value, you're a lot better off than you were before, so it's really a win-win situation for YOU, even though it's a losing situation for the poor soul who purchased your call.

Sadly, there is another possibility, that the stock price exceeds the strike price before the contract expires. In that case, you're required to sell the stock. You still end up in a position that isn't all that bad, however. You didn't lose any actual money, but you lost a potential profit. You still get the premium of $78, plus the earnings from the sale of the 100 shares at the strike price of $43.

A covered call is almost a zero-risk situation because you never actually lose money even though if the stock price soars, you obviously missed out on an opportunity. You can minimize that risk by choosing stocks you use for a covered call option carefully. For example, if you hold shares in a pharmaceutical company that is rumored to be announcing a cure for cancer in two months, you probably don't want to use those shares for a covered call. A company that has more long-term prospects but probably isn't going anywhere in the next few months is a better bet.

How to go about creating a covered call

To create a covered call, you'll need to own 100 shares of stock. While you don't want to risk a stock that is likely to take off in the near future, you don't want to pick a total dud either. There is always someone willing to buy something – at the right price. But you want to go with a decent stock so that you can earn a decent premium.

You start by getting online at your brokerage and looking up the stock online. When you look up stocks online, you'll be able to look at their "option chain" which will give you information from a table on premiums that are available for calls on this stock. You can see these listed under bid price. The bid price is given on a per share basis, but a call contract has 100 shares. If your bid price is $1.75, then the actual premium you're going to get is $1.75 x 100 = $175.

An important note is that the further out the expiration date, the higher the premium. A good rule of thumb is to pick an expiry that is between two and three months from the present date. Remember that the longer you go, the higher the risk because that increases the odds that the stock price will exceed the strike price and you'll end up having to sell the shares.

You have an option (no pun intended) with the premium you want to charge. Theoretically, you can set any price you want. Of course, that requires a buyer willing to pay that price for you to actually make the money. A more reasonable strategy is to look at prices people are currently requesting for call options on this stock. You can do this by checking the asking price for the call options on the stock. You can also see prices that buyers are currently offering by looking at the bid prices. For an instant sale, you can simply set your price to a bid price that is already out there. If you want to go a little bit higher, you can submit the order and then wait until someone comes along to buy your call option at the bid price.

To sell a covered call, you select "sell to open."

Benefits of Covered Calls

- A covered call is a relatively low-risk option. The worst-case scenario is that you'll be out of your shares but earn a small profit, a smaller profit than you could have made if you had not created the call contract and simply sold your shares. However, you also get the premium.

- A covered call allows you to generate income from your portfolio in the form of premiums.

- If you don't expect any price moves on the stock in the near term and you plan on holding it long term, it's a reasonable strategy to generate income without taking much risk.

Risks of Covered Calls

- Covered calls can be a risk if you're bullish on the stock, and your expectations are realized, and there is a price spike. In that case, you've traded the small amount of income of the premium with a voluntary cap of the strike price for the potential upside you could have had if you had simply held the stock and sold it at the high price.

- If the stock price plummets, while you still get the premium, the stocks will be worthless unless they rebound over the long term. You shouldn't use a call option on stocks that you expect to be on the path to a major drop in the coming months. In that case, rather than writing a covered call, you should simply sell the stocks and take your losses. Alternatively, you can continue holding the stocks to see if they rebound over the long term.

Chapter 13 Strategies for Buying Calls

I have urged you several times throughout this book to start paying attention to the stock market and learn how to spot trends in the ups and downs of particular shares. As you become increasingly familiar with that part of your options trading career, you can also make use of a column in the trading screen itself to guide you.

That column is titled "Open Interest" and it represents the total amount of open contracts on that particular underlying stock that are still running at the time you are viewing the page.

What you are looking at is the supply and demand on that stock. The more open interest on a particular contract, the more people believe it's a sure bet. You can also watch for sudden changes – if a call contract has 500 in that column one day and 2000 the next, it means that a significant number of traders believe that stock is going to move in that direction.

Those people aren't necessarily right, so it's up to you to use your judgment. Nevertheless, it can be a very helpful addition to your tool kit when it comes to predicting the movement of the stock market and making the right calls in your own trading.

At the same time, there are a number of factors that should be guiding you as you choose the right contract. As a call seller, you were mostly interested in the premium. As a buyer, you want a bargain. These factors include:

In or Out the Money: As a call seller, you were mostly interested in the premium. As a buyer, you want a bargain. You'll find that the premium is cheaper the more out of the money a contract is. In other words, the further the stock needs to climb before you can call in your option, the cheaper the premium will be. That doesn't mean it's the best bet – if you don't believe the stock will climb that high, it doesn't matter how cheap the premium is as you're not going to be able to purchase that stock. Calls that are slightly in the money are a good option for beginners and more likely to bring you a modest (or sometimes larger) profit.

Stock Movement: There is absolutely no point buying a bargain call that has a strike price higher than you believe it will go. If it never reaches that price, you've lost the premium you paid. Sometimes it can be worth the risk if you are reasonably sure the stock has a chance of rising that high, but not very often.

Time Value: If you're purchasing a contract that would require the stock to rise above a price, it stands to reason that you need to give it enough time to do that. Premiums also are lower on short term contracts, but that's because there's probably not enough time for the stock to reach its target. Be circumspect when looking for contracts with cheap premiums – the lowest price is often not the best one. It's important to give your strategy breathing room, so lean towards the calls with long enough expiration dates to allow the stock to do what you hope it will.

Spread: This is the difference between the bid and ask price and it has a direct impact on the price you will pay. A fair price usually falls somewhere between the two – the higher you pay, the more you are taking from your profit. Bear in mind that you will usually begin at a loss in your trade; if you pay $1.50 when the bid price was $1, that's a 50 cent loss on each share. As the whole idea is that the stock will rise in value, that's not necessarily a big issue – though it can be. As a general rule, if there is a wide spread, you should aim for somewhere in the middle. If it's narrow, you can probably pay the ask price without too much concern.

To make a profit buying covered calls, you have to be right on all these fronts. You need to choose the right time, the right direction and the right contract price if you're going to be successful. If you get one of these things wrong, you will likely lose that profit. Be aware that buying calls is where the risk comes in for options traders – which is why I highly recommend balancing your activity and relying on covered sells for your steady income, while keeping your buying activity relatively modest.

Chapter 14 Risk Management

Excellent risk management can save the worst trading strategy, but horrible risk management will sink even the best strategy. This is a lesson that many traders learn painfully over time, and I suggest you learn this by heart and install it deep within you even if you can't fully comprehend that statement.

Risk management has many different elements to both quantitative and qualitative. When it comes to options trading, the quantitative side is minimal thanks to the nature of options limiting risk by themselves. However, the qualitative side deserves a lot of attention. This chapter is going to give you the risk management framework that you need to succeed.

Risk

So what is risk anyway? Logically, it is the probability of you losing all of your money. In trading terms, you can think of it as being the probability of your actions putting you on a path to losing all of your capital. A good way to think about the need for good risk management is to ask yourself what a bad trader would do? Forget trading, what would a bad business person do with their capital?

Well, they would spend it on useless stuff that adds nothing to the bottom line. They would also increase expenses, market poorly, not take care of their employees, and be indiscipline with regards to their processes. While trading, you don't have employees or marketing needs, so you don't need to worry about that.

Do you have suppliers and costs? Well, yes, you do. Your supplier is your broker, and you pay fees to execute your trades. That is the cost of access. In directional trading, you have high costs as well because taking losses is a necessary part of trading. With market neutral or non-directional trading, your losses are going to be minimal, but you should still seek to minimize them.

What about discipline? Do you think you can trade and analyze the market well if you've just returned home from your job and are tired? If you didn't sleep properly last night? Or if you've argued with your spouse or partner? The point I'm making is that the more you behave like a terrible business owner, the more you increase your risk of failure.

Odds and Averages

Trading requires you to think a bit differently about profitability. In the previous paragraphs, I spoke about minimizing costs, and your first thought must have been to seek to reduce losses and maximize wins. This is a natural product of linear or ordered thinking. The market, however, is chaotic and linear thinking is going to get you nowhere.

Instead, you need to think in terms of averages and odds. Averages imply that you need to worry about your average loss size and your average win size. Seek to decrease the former and increase the latter. Notice that when we talk about averages, we're not necessarily talking about reducing the total number of losses. You can reduce the average by either reducing the sum of your losses or by increasing the number of losing trades while keeping the sum of the losses constant. This is a shift in thinking you must make.

Thinking in this way sets you up nicely to think in terms of odds, because in chaotic systems all you can bank on are odds playing out in the long run. For example, if you flip a coin, do you know in advance whether it's going to be a heads or tails? Probably not. But if someone asked you to predict the distribution of heads versus tails over 10,000 flips, you could reasonably guess that it'll be 5000 heads and 5000 tails. You might be off by a few flips either way, but you'll be pretty close percentage-wise.

In fact, the greater the number of flips, the lesser your error percentage. This is because the odds inherent in a pattern that occurs in a chaotic system express themselves best over the long run. Your trading strategy is precisely such a pattern. The market is a chaotic system. Hence, you should focus on executing your strategy as it is meant to be executed over and over again and worry about profitability only in the long run.

Contrast this with the usual attitude of traders who seek to win every single trade. This is impossible to accomplish since no trading strategy or pattern is correct 100% of the time. If we were discussing directional strategies, I'd spend a lot more time on this, but the fact is that options take care of a lot of this ambiguity themselves.

This is because you don't have to do much when trading options. You enter and then monitor the trade. Sure, it helps to have some directional bias, but even if you get it wrong, your losses will be extremely limited, and you're more likely to hit winners than losers.

Despite this, always think of your strategy in terms of its odds. There are two basic metrics to measure this. The first is the win rate of your system. This is simply the percentage of winners you have. The second is your payout ratio which is the average win size divided by the average loss size.

Together these two metrics will determine how profitable your system is. Both of them play off one another, and an increase in one is usually met by a decrease in another. It takes an extremely skillful trader to increase both simultaneously.

Risk Per Trade

The quantitative side of risk management when it comes to options trading is lesser than what you need to take care of when trading directionally. However, this doesn't mean there's nothing to worry about. Perhaps the most important metric of them all is your risk per trade. The risk per trade is what ultimately governs your profitability.

How much should you risk per trade? Common wisdom says that you should restrict this to 2% of your capital. For options trading purposes, this is perfectly fine. In fact, once you build your skill and can see opportunities better, I'd suggest increasing it to a higher level.

A point that you must understand here is that you must keep your risk per trade consistent for it to have any effect. You might see a wonderful setup and think that it has no chance of failure, but the truth is that you don't know how things will turn out. Even the prettiest setup has every chance of failing, and the ugliest setup you can think of may result in a profit. So never adjust your position size based on how something looks.

Calculating your position size for a trade is a pretty straightforward task. Every option's strategy will have a fixed maximum risk amount. Divide the capital risk by this amount, and that gives you your position size. Round that down to the nearest whole number since you can only buy whole number lots when it comes to contract sizes.

For example, let's say your maximum risk is $50 per lot on the trade. Your capital is $10,000. Your risk per trade is 2%. So the amount you're risking on that trade is 2% of 10,000 which is $200. Divide this by 50, and you get 4. Hence, your position size is four contracts or 400 shares. (You'll buy the contracts, not the shares.)

Why is it important to keep your risk per trade consistent? Well, recall that your average win and loss size is important when it comes to determining your profitability. These, in conjunction with your strategy's success rate, determine how much money you'll make. If you keep shifting your risk amount per trade, you'll shift your win and loss sizes. You might argue that since it's an average, you can always adjust amounts to reflect an average.

My counter to that is how would you know which trades to adjust in advance? You won't know which ones are going to be a win or a loss, so you won't know which trade sizes to adjust to meet the average. Hence, keep it consistent across all trades and let the math work for you.

Aside from risk per trade, there are some simple metrics you should keep track of as part of your quantitative risk management plan.

Drawdown

A drawdown refers to the reduction in capital your account experiences. Drawdowns by themselves always occur. The metrics you should be measuring are the maximum drawdown and recovery period. If you think of your account's balance as a curve, the maximum drawdown is the biggest peak to trough distance in dollars. The recovery period is the subsequent time it took for your account to make new equity high.

If your risk per trade is far too high, your max drawdown will be unacceptably high. For example, if you risk 10% per trade and lose two in a row, which is very likely, your drawdown is going to be 20%. This is an absurdly large hole to dig your way out. Consider that your capital has decreased by 20% and the subsequent climb back up needs to be done on lesser capital than previously.

This is why you need to keep your risk per trade low and in line with your strategy's success rate. The best way to manage drawdowns and limit the damage they cause is to put in place risk limits per day, week, and month. Even professional athletes who train to do one thing all the time have bad days, so it's unfair to expect yourself to be at 100% all the time.

These risk limits will take you out of the game when you're playing poorly. A daily risk limit is to prevent you from getting into a spiral of revenge trading. A good limit to stick to when starting off is to stop trading if you experience three losses in a row. This is pretty unlikely with options trades to be honest unless you screw up badly, but it's good to have a limit in place from a perspective of discipline.

Next, aim for a maximum weekly drawdown limit of 5% and a monthly drawdown limit of 6-8%. These are pretty high limits, to be honest, and if you are a directional trader, these limits do not apply to you. Directional traders need to be a lot more conservative than options trader when it comes to risk.

Understand that these are hard stop limits. So if your account has hit its monthly drawdown level within the first week, you need to take the rest of the month off. Overtrading and a lack of reflection on progress can cause a lot of damage, and a drawdown is simply a reflection of that.

Qualitative Risk

Quantitative metrics aside, your ability to properly manage qualitative things in your life and trading will dictate a lot of your success. Prepare well, and you're likely to see progress. You need to see preparation as your responsibility. I mean, no one else can prepare for you can they?

There are different elements to tracking your level of preparation so let's look at them one by one.

Health

You can't trade if you're physically unfit. If you have a fever or if you're suffering from some condition that makes it impossible for you to concentrate, forget about trading. You can rest assured that the other traders in the market will be more than happy to take your money.

When viewed from an options trading perspective, the risk is even more acute. All options strategies will require you to write options at some point, even the most basic ones like in this book. Even if your position is covered, making a mistake, and having an option you wrote be exercised by the buyer is an unpleasant thing that happens. Maintain a regimen of exercise and eat healthy food. Depending on how long you sit in front of your screen, you might even want to consider avoiding certain foods when in session.

Heavy meals and food that makes you drowsy will cause your performance to dip, so avoid eating them when you're in the market. Also, don't exercise to such an extent that you're completely exhausted. The idea is to be fresh and alert, not fatigued and aching for a good sleep.

You might have an image of traders as being highly wired and as people who spend their entire lives in front of a screen. Well, most traders do sit in front of a screen most of the time, but the successful ones make time for other stuff in their lives as well. So don't try to copy some false vision here. Instead, do what feels comfortable to you while taking care to not slip into habits that are detrimental to your success.

Lifestyle

Your fitness is just one part of your lifestyle, of course. Is your lifestyle conducive to profitable trading? Are you someone who loves staying up at all sorts of odd hours and considers it perfectly normal to stumble onto a work task while hungover or worse? Make no mistake, the market will make you donate all of your capital to it.

Many beginners underestimate how difficult trading is. This should come as no surprise since beginners by

174

definition underestimate anything. What shocks most of them is the degree to which they underestimate the difficulty of trading successfully. Let me put it in writing for you: Trading is one of the most challenging things you will ever do in your life.

The reason it is so difficult is due to the ever-changing nature of the market and the mental demands it places upon you. Another key lifestyle question to consider is the hours when you'll trade. Most of you reading this probably have full-time jobs and cannot spend your whole day in front of the market.

So plan out when you'll trade and how you'll prepare yourself for the session. What routines will you carry out? If you're going to trade in the morning before work begins, how will you manage to do this? Will you work in a quiet place or in some noisy truck stop on the way to work? Options positions don't need a lot of maintenance, so there's not much need for this, but when will you check in on the market throughout the day? Will you check in a few times? Five times? Define everything to do with your routine.

Think of yourself as a professional athlete who has to show up for a game everyday. An athlete has a precise method of preparation before showing up for a game. They don't deviate from their preparatory routine and certainly don't experiment with new things during game time. Practice is when they try out new stuff.

How will you practice your skills and improve your ability to execute your strategy? When will you do this? Plan it all out and develop your success routine.

Mental States

Trading is a mental activity. You don't need to lift or push anything physically. Therefore it is crucial to ensure that your mental state is as optimal as it needs to be for you to execute properly. Having a checklist or a mental check-in list works wonders for the trading process.

Before any trading, write down what's going through your mind and ask yourself how you feel. If you find that you're tired or frustrated and unable to focus properly, step away, and do not trade. If you're planning on sitting in front of your terminal for more than an hour, make it a habit to check in with yourself every half hour or hourly. This need not be a detailed examination, just a simple check-in with yourself to see how things are going.

Take your risk management tasks seriously, and the market will reward you with profits. Do not be the trader who stumbles into the market completely unprepared and then wonders why trading is so unforgiving. Above all else, seek to eliminate all sources of stress when it comes to trading. Take regular breaks and schedule months off from the market to recap and assimilate the things you've learned and need to improve.

Trading every single day of the year does not make sense. This isn't a job where you'll be rewarded with a certain salary for just showing up. You need to produce results, and in order to do so, you need to manage your downside carefully.

An excellent practice is to actually review how you work and set aside months exclusively for trading and months exclusively for practice purposes. By practice, I mean reviewing your prior results, working on your mindset and improving your risk management abilities. This is an unconventional method of working but it will pay massive dividends down the line.

Now that you have a better understanding of the basics, it's finally time to jump in and take a look at various trading strategies you can deploy with options.

Conclusion

After reading this book, you must have figured out how easy options trading is. With the information covered here plus your desire to make it in options trading, you have no option but to excel in the business. You are now better prepared to trade options using technical analysis, fundamental analysis, and other procedures. You are also ready to take opportunities as they come and have a sense of what each trade entails, from a technical view.

• An option refers to a contract that gives a buyer the authority to buy or sell an asset at a certain price within a certain period.

• Options do not represent the real value of an asset or underlying security. An option in itself is a derivative of an asset or security

• Calls give you the right to purchase an asset while puts allow you to sell an asset.

• The options market has four participants. These are the buyer of a call, the buyer of a put, the seller of a call and the seller of a put.

• The cost of an option is referred to as the premium.

- Long-term options are also known as leaps

By now, you understand that there are a good number of tools and platforms that you can use to trade options. Since the cost of options keeps fluctuating from the start date to the maturity date, you need a platform that best suits your trading and training needs. Bear in mind that each platform has its strengths and weaknesses; therefore, you may not find one that is 100 percent effective. A good platform is one that gives you the ability to tailor your experience. Such a platform can accommodate both novice and experienced traders. A sophisticated platform can negatively impact your proficiency since you will spend a considerable amount of time trying to understand the advanced tools and features on the platform. Having the right instrument will ensure that you trade with confidence.

Of course, we could not end the discussion without mentioning financial leverage as a benefit of trading options. The leverage comes about when you are able to translate your little capital into huge gains. It arises from the fact that a percentage increase in the price of an option is relatively higher than the increase in the underlying asset. This means that the more you invest, the higher the financial leverage. With a good trading plan, you can use this concept to minimize trading risks and maximize your returns. A great advantage in options trading is that the options contract itself is already a leverage opportunity. It allows you to grow your starting capital easily. By now, you should be able to calculate the leverage of any given position using the delta value.

When it comes to options trading, patience and commitment are key. You must be able to control your emotions. Emotional trading is a risky affair. Treating options like any other business can help manage losses with ease. Making trades just because they seem good can lead you into trouble. Actually, the difference between good traders and average ones is that a good trader does not allow emotions to control him. When he loses, he understands that it is because he made a wrong move or choice and that it is not the system that is working against him. Good traders do not dive into unnecessary opportunities just because of feelings; they weight the options and make decisions based on what is in the trade for them. They also understand when to quit from trade even if some losses are incurred.

We also looked at some of the tips you need to employ to ensure that you succeed in most of your trades if not all. These are simple things such as collecting enough capital before you start trading, identifying a suitable trading style, and having a risk management plan. You also have known some of the mistakes most traders make when trading options and how you can avoid them.

With all this insight into the options market, you should be able to carry out a trade from start to finish, successfully. You must, however, note that the options business is not for every investor. It can get sophisticated and dangerous if you do not put the information outlined in this book into practice.

By now, it is clear to you whether this is an investment you want to try out or not. If you are into it, then you must decide the kind of trader you would want to be. You can either be a day trader, long term trader, or a short-term trader. As a day trader, you will have the advantage of making several trades that close quickly. This option is good for you if you are interested in making small profits. Otherwise, consider long-term trading that can span a period of over 30 days but with incredible profits.

Trading on options also involves choosing the underlying security that you would wish to connect your options to. This may be in the form of commodities, stock, or foreign currency. Each currency has its own characteristics, and the liquidity status also matters. Commodities are good but very volatile, currencies trade most of the time, but the prices are easily influenced by economic news items. Stocks experience a rapid change in prices overnight.

To many people, options are a complicated instrument to trade in. However, the more you learn about them, the simpler they become. With some experience, you realize that the instrument is one of the most flexible to trade in. Nonetheless, for options trading to go well, you also need to understand the basics of picking a stock, assessing market cycles and formulating investment strategies.

Since options are highly volatile, if you do not exercise caution, you may lose all your investment at one go. That is why you need specialized training such as this one before venturing into it. A good number of people that have succeeded in options trading began as stock traders. If you are already into stock trading, you will have easy time trading options due to the many similarities that exist between the two.

Lastly, it is important to note that the shorter the trading period, the higher the stress and risks involved. If you keep holding your trades through the night, you stand a high risk of losing all your capital and destroying your account. Other than this, we are glad that you have learned a new way of earning money from the financial market and understood all the traits and skills you need to make it in binary options trading. Note that theory is never effective without practice. So, in case you need to get started, it is best to identify a trading platform and put what you have learned into practice. Remember, the more you practice, the more confident you become.

Made in the USA
Middletown, DE
14 February 2020

84794854R00104